IN SEARCH OF HEAVEN'S TRUTH: SEVEN GEMS

ARTHUR TAYLOR

BLUEROSE PUBLISHERS
India | U.K.

Copyright © Arthur Taylor 2024

All rights reserved by author. No part of this publication may be reproduced, stored in a retrieval system or transmitted in any form or by any means, electronic, mechanical, photocopying, recording or otherwise, without the prior permission of the author. Although every precaution has been taken to verify the accuracy of the information contained herein, the publisher assumes no responsibility for any errors or omissions. No liability is assumed for damages that may result from the use of information contained within.

BlueRose Publishers takes no responsibility for any damages, losses, or liabilities that may arise from the use or misuse of the information, products, or services provided in this publication.

For permissions requests or inquiries regarding this publication, please contact:

BLUEROSE PUBLISHERS
www.BlueRoseONE.com
info@bluerosepublishers.com
+91 8882 898 898
+4407342408967

ISBN: 978-93-6452-792-7

Cover design: Daksh
Typesetting: Tanya Raj Upadhyay

First Edition: October 2024

Preface

The creation of *In Search of Heaven's Truth: 7 Gems* was directed by the Spirit of God. It's coming forth was a 20-year journey in listening to its whisperings.

It is hoped that its review will bring each person closer to God along his or her journey for truth. The objective of 7 Gems is to enable the reader to review a simple summary of various religious texts, and then prayerfully consider with God one's own life and inward peace.

Peace is a gift from God, but must be sought for by individual faith, and choices consistent with one's own conscience.

The author takes no credit for the book. If it is divine, then it is from God. If not, then he leaves it to the judgment of all who may consider its pages.

Tribute to a Living Legend

Tribute To Revered Prof. Dr. Vishwanath Karad
MIT World Peace University | Prof. Dr. Vishwanath Karad | Pune

- Prof.(Dr.) Vishwanath D. Karad

Tribute to a Living Legend

When I think about what different world religions teach, I can only think of 'Peace, Love, Harmony, Respect for each other' and similar such words.

The essence & philosophy of all world religions is to 'Love & Let live'! Although billions of people across the world learn, read & practice various religions in their various forms, few practice them according to their true essence & philosophy. And one such person who actually does so, is Prof. Dr. Vishwanth D. Karad of Pune, Bharat!

He is endearingly & respectfully referred to as 'Vishwadharmi' which means a person who belongs to all world religions in letter and spirit! More than a hundred years ago, Swami Vivekananda of whom Prof. Karad is an ardent follower, had expressed his desire to see the youth of India giving shape to the rise of the nation. Revered Dr. Vishwanath D Karad read these words with his heart and soul. It had a profound effect on him. He showed the courage of conviction and breathed life into Swami Vivekananda's words.

He facilitated the progress of youth fully by creating Maharashtra Institute of Technology (now called MIT, Pune, India) in 1983. His focus lay on imparting holistic education to the students of MIT leading the youth to think and ponder upon the benefits of the pursuit of peace. This led to MIT being named as MIT World Peace University in 2017, where peace studies are a major part of its unique pedagogy.

Although a teacher and educationist by profession, Prof. Dr. Karad is truly one who practices 'omnism'. With a passion for conceptualizing, designing and creating monuments of excellence, all of his monuments and his activities reflect his strong belief in the oneness of the Almighty - the Ultimate Truth - the Ultimate Reality. His favourite tenet is 'Ekam Sat Vipra Bahudha Vadanti' from the Rigveda, which means, the

(Ultimate) Truth is only one, though scholarly people call it by different names.

These monuments convey the message of Universal Brotherhood and Peace. The brainchild of Revered Vishwanath Karad, the Philosopher Saint Dnyaneshwara World Peace Dome, World Peace Prayer Hall & Library, is an epitome of architectural magnificence and a contribution towards knowledge divine, an emblem of peace and a source of inspiration for all to embrace peace and humanitarian understanding. It depicts the Vedic principle articulated in Sanskrit as "Vasudhaiv Kutumbakam" (the World is one Family).

Needless to say Dr. Karad faced several numerous hurdles but he remained steadfast in his resolve to gift this architectural marvel and the message of peace for the future generations. Revered Prof. Dr. Vishwanath Karad's life mission to establish a 'Culture of Peace in the World' and deliverance of Value Based Universal Education are embodied in the establishment of World Peace Prayer Hall and World Peace Library. A living site of Interreligious peace and dialogue, the World Peace Dome constructed at the picturesque Vishwarajbaug, Pune, is not only the largest dome in the world but a living heritage of harmonious amalgamation of eastern spiritual peace and western scientific wisdom exemplifying the ethos of 'Vasudhaiva Kutumbakam'- 'The World is One family.

The magnificent structure with 160 ft. diameter and 263 ft height contains 54 larger-than-life-size bronze statues of many outstanding Saints, Scientists and Philosophers from Saint Dnyaneshwar to Albert Einstein. It is an embodiment of establishing a culture of peace and sustainable development that are at the heart of UNESCO's mandate. I therefore, consider this as my sacred duty to pay tributes to this outstanding personality, a living legend, Prof. Dr. Vishwanath D. Karad, who is a true Beacon of Light in this world full of anarchy and disorder.

[Attribution and thanks to MIT-World Peace University for this Tribute and use of photos.]

Introduction

This book, *In Search of Heaven's Truth: 7 Gems,* is a first-of-its-kind, setting forth the basic teachings of multiple religious texts, all in one place.

Accordingly, the holy writings behind Judaism, Christianity, Islam, Hinduism, and Buddhism are all set forth in one book. Multiple faiths follow these texts. Accordingly, this book does not attempt to describe any of these faiths themselves, or beliefs of those who follow these texts. Instead, it merely recites what the texts themselves say.

Over a period of some 20 years, the language of each text was intricately reviewed. Each verse of every text was separately reviewed for concepts and, with the use of modern technology, *In Search of Heaven's Truth: 7 Gems* (this book) and *Religious Digests* setting forth over 80,000 textual references by topic (to be published separately) were created.

Religious Digests thus provide prolific documentation for *In Search of Heaven's Truth: 7 Gems*. A small portion of the *Religious Digests'* references—a few thousand--are included in the book as endnotes.

The objective of *In Search of Heaven's Truth: 7 Gems* is simply to present basics of each of the seven texts for the billions who may have never read or considered them, and to provide the reader with a very credible and carefully documented understanding. A greater understanding and respect of the followers of different religious texts will inevitably follow.

Five of these texts come from Abrahamic faiths (Judaism, Christianity, and Islam.) Two of them come from non-Abrahamic faiths (Hinduism and Buddhism.)

The Torah is the most widely believed of all the religious texts, and is thus the text most accepted throughout the entire world. Accepted by

Jews, Muslims, and Christians, The Torah's believers exceed 4.5 billion people—more than half the world's entire population.

In Search of Heaven's Truth: 7 Gems is written for a world-wide audience of Jews, Christians, Muslims, Hindus, and Buddhists alike, as well as for those of yet other faiths, or no faith at all.

For simplicity's sake, the Nevi'im and Ketuvim, while distinct religious texts, are nevertheless combined with the Torah.

All persons of all faiths are invited to pursue their own spiritual journey for truth and peace. May all mankind respect the spiritual writings of those of other faiths, and in the process, increase world unity.

Electronic Links

(For those desiring to read any portion of any of the texts, or to read a particular endnote, a listing of electronic links to free copies of all the texts is provided below. These links were all active and operable as of the time of this printing.)

The Law (Torah)
https://jps.org/wp-content/uploads/2015/10/Tanakh1917.pdf

The Prophets, Ancient (Nevi'im)
https://jps.org/wp-content/uploads/2015/10/Tanakh1917.pdf

The Writings (Ketuvim)
https://jps.org/wp-content/uploads/2015/10/Tanakh1917.pdf

Holy Bhagavad Gita
https://bhagavadgita.io

Book of Mormon: Another Testament of Jesus Christ
https://www.churchofjesuschrist.org/study/scriptures/bofm?lang=eng

New Testament of Jesus Christ
https://www.churchofjesuschrist.org/study/scriptures/nt?lang=eng

Native Indigenous Writings
https://www.gutenberg.org/files/340/340-h/340-h.htm

Holy Quran (Islam)
https://blog.clearquran.com/download/

Principal Upanishads (Hindu)
https://www.holybooks.com/wp-content/uploads/The-Ten-Principal-Upanishads.pdf

Dead Sea Scrolls (Bible Translations)
Biblical Dead Sea Scrolls (dssenglishbible.com)

Sutra Pitaka (Buddhist)
Sutta Pitaka: The Basket of Suttas (accesstoinsight.org)

The Prophets, Modern
https://www.churchofjesuschrist.org/general-conference?lang=eng

Sri Guru Granth Sahib (Sikh)
https://www.sikhnet.com/Siri-Guru-Granth-Sahib#tab-read

Tao Te Ching (Taoism)
https://www.poetryintranslation.com/klineastao.php

Apocrypha
http://www.scriptural-truth.com/apocrypha_books.html

Copyright 2024 by Arthur Taylor

All rights reserved

Table of Contents

Chapter 1
Torah (With Nevi'im and Ketuvim) 1

Chapter 2
Shrimad Bhagavad Gita 39

Chapter 3
The Book of Mormon: Another Testament of Jesus Christ 55

Chapter 4
New Testament of Jesus Christ 71

Chapter 5
The Holy Qur'an 93

Chapter 6
Modern Prophets 113

Chapter 7
The Sutra Pitakas (Limited) 127

CHAPTER 1

Torah
(With Nevi'im and Ketuvim)

Torah

The Torah consists of five books of Moses: Genesis, Exodus, Leviticus, Numbers, and Deuteronomy.

The Nevi'im and Ketuvim consist of multiple other writings of ancient prophets, including Isaiah, Jeremiah, Amos, and Malachi.

Some believe the Torah was direct revelation from God to Moses, which he recorded and has been passed down in written form now for centuries.

The Torah is perhaps the most widely accepted of all religious texts today, and is cited in part in the additional religious texts of the Book of Mormon,[1] the New Testament,[2] the Quran,[3] and Modern Prophets.[4]

The Torah tells of the creation of the earth,[5] the placement of Adam and Eve upon it in the Garden of Eden as its first inhabitants,[6] the transgressions of Adam and Eve in partaking of the forbidden fruit[7] and their being thrust out of the Garden of Eden by God into the world.[8]

The Torah tells of Adam and Eve's first children,[9] and of the jealousy of Cain[10] and his subsequent decision to slay his brother, Abel.[11]

Abraham and Obedience

It speaks of a righteous descendant of Adam, named Abraham,[12] who followed God and, in turn, received promises from God that he would have a great posterity[13] as well as lands[14] that God would give to him as an inheritance.

It also tells of Abraham's son, named Isaac,[15] and grandson, named Jacob[16] who also were faithful followers of God.

One event tells of Abraham and Isaac as Abraham went to offer sacrifices to the Lord. God had commanded Abraham to offer his son Isaac as that sacrifice.[17] Abraham rose up early in the morning[18] to go and do as God had directed.

Upon arrival at their destination Isaac asked where the offering animal was,[19] and then, seemingly without resistance, submitted to God's will as Abraham informed him that he, Isaac, was to be sacrificed to God.[20]

At the very moment when Abraham was to slay his son an angel appeared to him[21] and forbid him from doing so.[22] Isaac was released and a ram that had become caught in the thicket was then sacrificed to God instead.[23]

Abraham thus passed the test of God of his devotion to Him and his willingness to even offer his own beloved son in order to follow God's commandments.[24]

Many Christian followers of the Torah believe that this event was instructive to Abraham, and perhaps Isaac also, of God's future offering of His own Beloved Son, Jesus Christ.[25]

Joseph and Forgiveness

The Torah tells of Israel's twelve sons,[26] including one named Joseph.[27] God gave Joseph dreams revealing to Him that one day his family would bow in obeisance to him.[28]

Joseph was highly favored of his father, Israel.[29] Jealousy among his brothers rose to the point when one day while some distance from home they staged the fake death of Joseph, stripped Joseph of his coat, and placed animal blood upon his garment.[30] They then carried the torn and bloodied coat to Joseph's father, Israel, and told him that Joseph had been killed by wild beasts.[31] In fact, he had not been slain, but they had sold him as a slave to a caravan of travelers.[32]

That caravan carried Joseph into Egypt where Joseph rose in prominence and in trial as he faithfully served his masters, and despite his being thrown into prison on false charges[33] he continued his devotion to God and his loyal service to mankind.[34]

God gave to Joseph dreams[35] which showed to others God's inspiration and trust in Him.

The Torah tells how Joseph interpreted another dream—this one of Pharaoh—and that there would be seven years of prosperity in the land, and then seven years of famine.[36]

Thereafter Joseph became the right-hand man to Pharaoh who gave him charge of all his doings in Egypt.[37]

Joseph helped all of Egypt preserve food during the years of plenty that they would have enough during the times of famine.[38]

Meanwhile, the Torah indicates, Israel and Joseph's brothers began to suffer because of the drought.[39] Most of the brothers came to Egypt to obtain food.[40]

As the result of divine direction, they ended up seeking food before the presence of Joseph, now a grown man and a ruler in Egypt. They did not recognize him or know that he was their brother.[41]

Over a period of days Joseph used his authority to cause delays in their return with food to their father. He accused them of being spies, and held one of them as ransom until the others would go and then return again with their youngest brother, Benjamin, whom they had mentioned to Joseph in their earlier discussions, as proof that they in fact were not spies.[42]

Despite Israel's great reluctance to allow his brothers to take Benjamin down to Egypt, he eventually relented as they went again for more food and to prove that they were not spies.[43]

When all the brothers came again, Joseph—still unrevealed to them as their brother—provided a meal for them.[44] He sat them all in order of age which stunned his brothers.[45] He caused that Benjamin, whom he loved, should be served five times the amount of everyone else.[46]

Then Joseph sent them away again but, unbeknownst to the brothers, had his silver cup placed in the sack of Benjamin.[47] The sons were all returned to Joseph's presence where he ordered that the person (Benjamin) in whose sack the silver cup had been found should be kept there, while the others could return to their father.[48] Judah then plead for Benjamin, saying that if they returned without him that Israel, the boy's father, would die.[49] Judah offered that he be kept instead of Benjamin.[50]

The Torah tells one of the most touching accounts as Joseph, no longer able to refrain his affections for his family, cast all the Egyptians from the banquet hall.[51] He then in a tearful if not sacred moment revealed to his brothers, who decades earlier had betrayed him and sold him into servitude, that he was in fact Joseph, their brother.[52]

The Torah tells that they were troubled at his presence.[53] Nevertheless, Joseph comforted them and freely forgave them of their prior treacherous deeds. Instead, he said it was the divine grace of God that had allowed those events to happen so that in a future time Joseph would be in a position to bless and protect his own family.[54]

Moses and Deliverance

Israel's posterity grew in Egypt, until generations later, and with a different Pharaoh, all of the descendants as a people, called Israel because of the name of their forefather, were placed in servitude to Pharaoh and Egypt.[55]

They were no longer in Egypt as a place of refuge, but now were there as a place of bondage.

The Torah tells of God's commands to Moses to go to Pharaoh and tell him that God commanded him now to let Israel go.[56] Pharaoh refused, and over a series of many encounters God sent plagues of lice and locusts, turned all the water to blood—all in an attempt to persuade Pharaoh to comply.[57]

But Pharaoh still refused.[58]

Finally, God sent Moses to Pharaoh to tell him that all the first-born of Egypt would be slain—the first-born of animals as well as the first-born of Pharaoh himself.[59]

Pharaoh still refused.[60]

So God slew all the first-born of Egypt as He had warned He would do.[61] But in an act of divine mercy, He instructed Moses to tell Israel to protect themselves from this promised death. If Israel would mark the posts of their homes with lamb's blood, then when the angel of death came he would "pass over" that house and not slay any first-born inside.[62]

Israel did so and was thus protected.[63] God's miraculous and selective judgment upon the Egyptians for refusing His word, and His divine protection upon Israel for humbly following His word has been marked and remembered ever since as a holy day called Passover.[64]

Many Christian followers of other religious texts see the Passover as a symbol of the saving power of the Lamb of God, Jesus Christ.[65]

Israel and the Armies of Egypt

Pharaoh relented and let Israel leave Egypt, which they did.[66] But on their way towards the Red Sea Pharaoh had an apparent change of heart and sent Egyptian forces to slay Israel in the wilderness.[67]

Weaponless and up against the Red Sea, Israel was defenseless against the oncoming Egyptians.[68] But as they plead to God and Moses for deliverance, God told Moses to command the Red Sea to open up.[69] It did.[70] Forward-flowing waters were stopped; the entire sea was divided. The ground at the bottom of the Sea was made dry, and Israel en-masse made their escape across the Red Sea before the Egyptian armies arrived.[71]

Determined to destroy Israel, the armies followed after Israel down into the now dry river bed. However, as they did so God closed up the Red

Sea and the waters returned to their normal flow and all the armies of the Egyptians were destroyed.[72]

Israel had been miraculously saved by the hand of God.[73]

God Appears to Moses; The Ten Commandments

Israel traveled into the wilderness with the hope of entering Palestine, a land promised to them from God.[74]

While in the wilderness Moses went up unto God into the Mount of Sanai.[75]

There the mount was "altogether on a smoke" and the "whole mount quaked greatly."[76]

God wrote His words upon tablets which Moses then took down the Mount to Israel.[77]

However, when he drew near to Israel he quickly learned that they were in a state of open rebellion against God, and had at the insistence of the people made a golden calf which they worshipped.[78]

Moses deeply frustrated at the lack of humility and obedience of Israel broke the tablets which God had given, perhaps understanding that they were not fit for a people so rebellious.[79]

Moses subsequently went up to Mount Sanai again. He again communed with God. God gave him a second set of tablets with His words, perhaps a simpler version with a lesser law tailored for a weaker people.[80]

These words on these tablets are known as the Ten Commandments and are recorded in the Torah in Exodus chapter 20.[81]

God through the Ten Commandments commands Israel to have no other gods before Him, to make no graven images nor to bow down to them, to not take His name in vain, not kill, not commit adultery, not steal, not bear false witness, not covet, to honor their father and their mother, and to keep the Sabbath Day holy.[82]

Festivals

The Torah speaks of multiple festivals Israel is commanded to remember and celebrate such as for the Passover, the feast of ingathering, the feast of tabernacles, and the feast of unleavened bread.[83] These feasts are "holy convocations."[84] Passover reminds Israel of God's mercy in passing over them at the time that all the firstborn of Egypt were slain. They also remind Israel of God's mercy in granting them another yearly harvest.

Unclean

The Torah describes many potential dietary practices of Israel as "unclean" and forbids them from engaging in them. Among these is the admonition to not eat pork,[85] nor blood,[86] camel,[87] coney,[88] that which dieth of itself,[89] creeping things that flieth,[90] the eagle,[91] vulture,[92] hawk,[93] owl,[94] raven,[95] mouse,[96] the tortoise.[97] Neither should one seeth a kid in its mother's milk[98] (which gives rise to the Kosher practice of not mixing meat and milk.)

In addition to dietary practices which may have been unhealthy then, the Torah also describes other life circumstances which cause an individual to be "unclean",[99] such as that found during a woman's monthly cycle.[100]

The Torah sets forth what an individual who is unclean must do to become clean again.[101]

Messiah

The Torah, Nevi'im, and Ketuvim speak of a Messiah who is to come. There are two distinct groupings of these scriptures. One group speaks of the Messiah's Glorious Coming with glory,[102] fire,[103] judgement,[104] destruction,[105] as He descends with righteous saints[106] and rules as King over all the earth.[107]

The other grouping speaks of the Messiah's Mortal Coming with (a) a virgin conceiving,[108] the birth of the Mighty God as a child,[109] coming as a descendant of Jacob out of Bethlehem;[110] (b) events of His life as He is called out of Egypt,[111] raised up,[112] with no beauty,[113] with a voice preparing the way before Him,[114] who rides upon an ass,[115] and is betrayed by a friend[116] for thirty pieces of silver;[117] (c) suffering as He is wounded for our transgressions,[118] gives His back to the smiter[119] (and also His cheek),[120] is brought to the slaughter as a lamb;[121] and (d) hands being pierced,[122] being "cut off",[123] and dying with the wicked,[124] with lots then cast upon His garment.[125]

It is these Mortal Coming scriptures in the Torah, Nevi'im and Ketuvim that define the difference between those of the Christian, Muslim, and Jewish faiths.

- **Christian Faith**

Those of the Christian faith believe that Jesus Christ has already fulfilled the Mortal Coming prophecies, and will yet fulfill the Glorious Coming prophecies.

- **Muslim Faith**

Those of the Muslim faith believe that Jesus Christ was a prophet, but do not believe he was the Son of God.

- **-Jewish Faith**

Those of the Jewish faith believe that there is only one coming to occur of the Messiah—the Glorious Coming—and look forward to it.

Christians believe that the prophecies of the Mortal Coming will occur first, and of the Glorious Coming second. They believe reversing the sequence is impossible—for the Messiah to come with glory, judgment and destruction first, and then subsequently be born, called out of Egypt, ride upon an ass, suffer, be brought to the slaughter as a lamb, and then die.

Of great interest to all faiths are three verses in Zechariah[126] which connect the Glorious Coming to the Mortal Coming, describing a triumphal defense of Jerusalem inhabitants by the Messiah (Glorious Coming) and the ensuing discussion about wound marks in his hands (Mortal Coming) and a realization, regret and bitterness that follow.[127]

Mortal Coming Details

Spread throughout the Torah, Nevi'im and Ketuvim are some 50 separate scriptures describing the Messiah's Mortal Coming. These passages (without endnotes, but with in-text references shown below) reference His birth, life, miracles, Atonement, crucifixion, and resurrected body. Such passages include references to a virgin conceiving, that He would be called out of Egypt, one would prepare the way before Him, He would speak in parables, no deceit would come from His mouth, He would bind up the broken hearted, and He would ride triumphantly upon the foal of an ass into Jerusalem.

In addition, these Torah, Nevi'im, and Ketuvim passages prophecy that the Messiah would be the Stone the builders refused, still the waves and calm the storm, be afflicted in all their afflictions, stricken and wounded for their transgressions, and betrayed and sold for exactly the price of 30 pieces of silver.

Finally, these 50 prophecies of the Messiah state that the Messiah would be a Lamb brought to the slaughter, that His hands would be pierced, that He would be mocked, that His oppressors would wag their heads at Him, but not one bone would be broken in His body, and that lots would be cast upon his clothing.

Mortal Coming Fulfillment

The New Testament records the fulfilment of each of these 50 scriptures.

A description of these 50 prophecies is here listed. Then, the actual Torah, Nevi'im, Ketuvim, and New Testament references follow below:

- **Messiah's Birth and Youth:**

Virgin shall conceive;
Ruler come out of Bethlehem;
Rachel weeping for her children, they were not;
Call my Son out of Egypt;
Star out of Jacob;
Righteous Branch;
Stem of Jesse;
Raise up a Prophet;
Prince of Peace;

- **Messiah's Teachings and Ministry:**

Prepare ye the way of the Lord, crieth in the wilderness;
Put my spirit upon my servant;
Open His mouth in parables;
No deceit in His mouth;
Land of Zebulun and Naphtali, seen a great light;
Walked in darkness, saw a great light;
Hear, understand not, see, perceive not;
Bind up the broken hearted;
Thy King cometh;
King cometh, riding upon an ass;

Precious cornerstone;
The stone builders refused;

- **Messiah's Miracles:**

Waves stilled;
Storm calmed;

- **Messiah's Suffering:**

Afflicted in all their afflictions;
Bruised him;
Stricken for the transgressions of His people;
Wounded for transgressions;
Borne our griefs, carried our sorrows;

- **Messiah's Betrayal to Death:**

Friend "lifted up his heel";
Sold for silver;
Thirty pieces of silver;
Hated without a cause;
Lamb brought to the slaughter;
Smite the Shepherd, sheep are scattered;
Gave back to the smiters;
Giveth His cheek;
Smiteth him;
Nail in His holy, sure place;
Hands pierced;
Numbered with the transgressors;
Mocked, "let him deliver him";
Mocked, "wag his head";
Given vinegar to drink;
"My God, my God, why hast thou forsaken" me;
Into God's hand commits His spirit;
Pierced;

Not one bone is broken;
His garments will be parted; Lots cast upon His vesture;
Grave with the wicked; and,
Cut off.

Here are the references for each of these 50 Torah, Nevi'im and Ketuvim prophecies, as well as their New Testament fulfillment:

(#) Prophecy / Fulfillment	Book	Chapter	Verse
(1) a virgin shall conceive	Isaiah	7	14
virgin shall be with child…bring forth a son…call his name Emmanuel…interpreted…God with us	Matthew	1	23
(2) thou, Bethlehem..though thou be little…out of thee shall he come forth…ruler in Israel	Micah	5	2
thou Bethlehem…art not the least among the princes of Juda…come a Governor…rule	Matthew	2	6
(3) in Ramah, lamentation, and bitter weeping; Rachel weeping for her children…they were not	Jeremiah	31	15
Herod…slew all the children that were in Bethlahem	Matthew	2	16
(4) I loved him, and called my son out of Egypt	Hosea	11	1
was there until the death of Herod…fulfilled which was spoken…Out of Egypt…called my son	Matthew	2	15
(5) come a Star out of Jacob	Numbers	24	17
Jesus Christ	Matthew	1	1
Abraham begat Isaac…begat Jacob…Judah…Phares	Matthew	1	2

Page | 13

(6) righteous Branch	Jeremiah	23	5
Jesus Christ	Matthew	1	1
(7) stem of Jesse	Isaiah	11	1
Jesus Christ	Matthew	1	1
Salmon begat Booz of Rachab…Booz begat Obed of Ruth…Obed begat Jesse	Matthew	1	5
And Jesse begat David the king; and David the king begat Solomon	Matthew	1	6
(8) The Lord thy God will raise up unto thee a Prophet from the midst…hearken	Deuteronomy	18	15
Prophet…like unto thee	Deuteronomy	18	18
The woman saith unto him, Sir, I perceive that thou art a prophet	John	4	19
(9) his name shall be called…Prince of Peace	Isaiah	9	6
let not your heart be troubled, neither let it be afraid	John	14	27
(10) voice of him…crieth in the wilderness, Prepare ye the way of the Lord, make straight	Isaiah	40	3
one crying in the wilderness, Prepare ye the way of the Lord, make his paths straight	Luke	3	4
writen in the prophets…I send my messenger…prepare thy way before thee	Mark	1	2
voice of one crying in the wilderness, Prepare ye the way of the Lord…paths straight	Mark	1	3
(11) To open the blind eyes, to bring out the prisoners from the prison	Isaiah	42	7
Behold my servant…beloved…put my spirit upon him…he shall shew judgment…Gentiles	Matthew	12	18

(12) I will open my mouth in a parable	Psalm	78	2
Watch ye therefore: for ye know not when the master of the house cometh	Mark	13	35
(13) neither was any deceit in his mouth	Isaiah	53	9
I am the way…truth…life: no man cometh unto the Father, but by me	John	14	6
(14) land of Zebulun…land of Naphtali…people walked in darkness have seen a great light	Isaiah	9	1
he came and dwelt in Capernaum…in the borders of Zabulon and Nephthalim	Matthew	4	13
might be fulfilled…Esaias…land of Zabulon…Nephthalim…people…saw great light	Matthew	4	14
The land of Zabulon, and the land of Nephtalim, by the way of the sea	Matthew	4	15
(15) walked in darkness…see a…light	Isaiah	9	2
The people which sat in darkness saw great light	Matthew	4	16
(16) Hear ye indeed, but understand not…see ye indeed, but perceive not	Isaiah	6	9
prophecy of Esaias…hearing ye shall hear…not understand…seeing…see...not perceive	Matthew	13	14
(17) he hath sent me to bind up the brokenhearted, to proclaim liberty to the captives	Isaiah	61	1
Neither do I condemn thee: go, and sin no more	John	8	11
(18) behold, thy King cometh unto thee	Zechariah	9	9
hosanna: Blessed is the King of Israel	John	12	13

Behold, thy King cometh unto thee, meek, and sitting upon an ass, and a colt	Matthew	21	5
they that followed, cried, saying, Hosanna; Blessed is he that cometh in the name…Lord	Mark	11	9
Blessed be the kingdom of our father David, that cometh in the name of the Lord: Hosanna	Mark	11	10
(19) riding upon an ass, and upon a colt	Zechariah	9	9
Jesus, when he had found a young ass, sat thereon	John	12	14
ass…colt…hosanna	Matthew	21	7
ye shall find a colt tied, whereon never man sat; loose him, and bring him	Mark	11	2
(20) precious corner stone	Isaiah	28	16
The stone which the builders rejected…same is become the head of the corner	Matthew	21	42
(21) stone…builders refused	Psalm	118	22
The stone which the builders rejected…same is become the head of the corner	Matthew	21	42
This is the stone which was set at nought of you builders…become…head…corner	Acts	4	11
(22) waves…thou stillest them	Psalm	89	9
peace, be still…wind ceased, and there was a great calm	Mark	4	39
(23) he maketh the storm a calm	Psalm	107	29
peace, be still…wind ceased, and there was a great calm	Mark	4	39
(24) Saviour…he bare them, and carried them all the days of old	Isaiah	63	9
his sweat was as it were great drops of blood falling down to the ground	Luke	22	44

(25) pleased the Lord to bruise him	Isaiah	53	10
shewed by…prophets…Christ should suffer, he hath so fulfilled	Acts	3	18
(26) for the transgression of my people was he stricken	Isaiah	53	8
his sweat was as it were great drops of blood falling down to the ground	Luke	22	44
(27) he was wounded for our transgressions	Isaiah	53	5
his sweat was as it were great drops of blood falling down to the ground	Luke	22	44
(28) Surely he hath borne our griefs, and carried our sorrow	Isaiah	53	4
Esaias…Himself took our infirmities, and bare our sicknesses	Matthew	8	17
(29) mine…friend…lifted up his heel	Psalm	41	9
Then one of the twelve, called Judas Iscariot, went unto the chief priests	Matthew	26	14
(30) sold the righteous for silver	Amos	2	6
thirty pieces of silver	Matthew	26	15
(31) So they weighed for my price thirty pieces of silver	Zechariah	11	12
(31) And I took the thirty pieces of silver, and cast them to the potter in the house of the Lord	Zechariah	11	13
fulfilled…Jeremy the prophet…they took the thirty pieces of silver, the price	Matthew	27	9
(32) They that hate me without a cause	Psalm	69	6
fulfilled that is written in their law, They hated me without a cause	John	15	25
(33) I was like a lamb or an ox that is brought to the slaughter	Jeremiah	11	19
Caiaphas	Matthew	26	57
(34) smite the shepherd, and the sheep shall be scattered	Zechariah	13	7
Then all the disciples forsook him	Matthew	26	56

And they all forsook him, and fled	Mark	14	50
be offended because of me this night..I will smite the shepherd…sheep…scattered	Matthew	14	27
be offended because of me this night…written…smite the shepherd…scattered	Matthew	26	31
(35) gave my back to the smiters	Isaiah	50	6
released he Barabbas unto them…scourged Jesus…delivered him to be crucified	Matthew	27	26
Pilate, willing to content the people, released Barabbas…Jesus..scourged him…crucified	Mark	15	15
Pilate therefore took Jesus, and scourged him	John	19	1
(36) he giveth his cheek	Lamentations	3	30
they spit in his face, and buffeted him…others smote him with the palms…hands	Matthew	26	67
(37) smiteth him	Lamentations	3	30
they spit in his face, and buffeted him…others smote him with the palms…hands	Matthew	26	67
(38) nail in his holy place	Ezra	9	8
(38) nail in a sure place	Isaiah	22	23
(38) out of him came forth…the nail	Zechariah	10	4
I shall see in his hands the print of the nails, and put my finger into the print of the nails	John	20	25
(39) they pierced my hands	Psalm	22	16
I shall see in his hands the print of the nails, and put my finger into the print of the nails	John	20	25

(40) he was numbered with the transgressors	Isaiah	53	12
scripture was fulfilled…he was numbered with the transgressors	Mark	15	28
(41) He trusted on the Lord that he would deliver him: let him deliver him	Psalm	22	8
Save thyself, and come down from the cross	Mark	15	30
Likewise also the chief priests mocking said…with the scribes…saved others; himself	Mark	15	31
(42) wag his head	Jeremiah	18	16
they that passed by railed on him, wagging their heads	Mark	15	29
Save thyself, and come down from the cross	Mark	15	30
(43) They gave me also gall for my meat; and in my thirst they gave me vinegar to drink	Psalm	69	21
one ran and filled a spunge full of vinegar, and put it on a reed, and gave him to drink	Mark	15	34
(44) my God, my God, why hast thou forsaken	Psalm	22	1
Jesus cried with a loud voice…"My God, my God, why hast thou forsaken me?"	Mark	15	36
(45) into thine hand I commit my spirit	Psalm	31	5
Father, into thy hands I commend my spirit	Luke	23	46
(46) they shall look upon me whom they have pierced	Zechariah	12	10
They shall look on him whom they pierced	John	19	37
(47) He keepeth all his bones: not one of them is broken	Psalm	69	21

scripture should be fulfilled, A bone of him shall not be broken	John	19	36
(48) They part my garments among them, and cast lots upon my vesture	Psalm	22	18
they parted his raiment, and cast lots	Luke	23	34
fulfilled…parted my garments among them...upon my vesture did they cast lots	Matthew	27	35
they had crucified him, they parted his garments, casting lots upon them	Mark	15	24
scripture might be fulfilled…They parted my raiment among them…my vesture…cast lots	John	19	24
(49) he made his grave with the wicked…neither was any deceit in his mouth	Isaiah	53	9
with him they crucify two thieves; the one on his right hand, and the other on his left	Mark	15	27
(50) Messiah be cut off	Daniel	9	26
Father, into thy hands I commend my spirit	Luke	23	46

The other references to the Messiah in the Torah, Nevi'im, and Ketuvim refer to the Messiah's Glorious Coming, as outlined above, and not His Mortal Coming.

- **Jesus Christ, Summary**

Those of the Christian faith believe the remarkable fulfillment of these 50 scriptures comes in the Person, Jesus Christ of Nazareth.[128]

The New Testament is thus a sequel to the prophetic writings which preceded it. It is the natural sequel to the Torah, Nevi'im, and Ketuvim.

They believe it is a witness, or Testament—a New Testament—that the Messiah prophesied in the Torah, Nevi'im, and Ketuvim has in fact been sent by God to earth. It is thus a witness that Jesus Christ is the Messiah, the actual divine Son of God the Father.[129]

The Book of Mormon is also a witness, "Another Testament", that the prophecies of the Torah, Nevi'im, and Ketuvim[130] and of the coming Messiah and Redeemer[131] are indeed true, and that Jesus Christ is the promised Messiah[132] and will yet come in His glorious return.[133]

The Atonement

The Torah speaks extensively of blood and atonement. It states that,

"[B]lood…maketh an Atonement for the soul."[134]

In addition to the soul, the land also can be cleansed by the blood:

"[T]he land cannot be cleansed of the blood that is shed therein, but by the blood of him that shed it."[135]

Priestly practices thus frequently used blood in their sacrifices. One example with the "sin offering" is as follows:

"And the priest shall take of the blood of the sin offering with his finger, and put it upon the horns of the altar of burnt offering, and shall pour out all the blood thereof at the bottom of the altar…."[136]

The Book of Mormon, New Testament, and Modern Prophets teaches that this blood sacrificed of animals was symbolic of the blood which would later be sacrificed by Jesus Christ for the sins of all mankind.[137]

- **Messiah would suffer for our Sins**

The Torah, Nevi'im, and Ketuvim prophecy that the Messiah would suffer and take upon Him the sins of His people:

"Lord hath laid on him the iniquity of us all."[138]

"[H]e shall bear their iniquities."[139]

"[F]or the transgression of my people was he stricken."[140]

- **Messiah would also suffer for our Pains and Afflictions**

Isaiah prophesied that in addition to suffering for sins, the Messiah also would suffer for the pains and heartaches of every person ever to live upon the earth.

"[I]n all their affliction he was afflicted...."[141]
"Surely he hath borne our griefs, and carried our sorrow...."[142]
"[W]ith his stripes we are healed...."[143]

Crucifixion and Death

The Torah, Nevi'im, and Ketuvim speak of the Messiah's crucifixion and death. These prophets state,

"[T]hey shall look upon me whom they have pierced, and they shall mourn for him."[144]
"What are these wounds in thine hands?"[145]
"[O]ut of him came forth...the nail...."[146]
"[N]either shall ye break a bone...."[147]
"So they weighed for my price thirty pieces of silver...."[148]

Resurrection

Multiple prophecies in the Nevi'im and Ketuvim tell of the resurrection. Among them are the following:

"[E]arth shall cast out the dead..."[149]
"I will bring sinews upon you, and will bring up flesh upon you, and cover you with skin..."[150]
"I will ransom them from the power of the grave: I will redeem them from death."[151]

The following prophecies of Isaiah and Job are particularly specific:

> *"Thy dead men shall live, together with my dead body shall they arise. Awake and sing, ye that dwell in dust: for thy dew is as the dew of herbs, and the earth shall cast out the dead."*[152]
>
> *"If a man die, shall he live again?...For I know that my redeemer liveth, and that he shall stand at the latter day upon the earth: And though after my skin worms destroy this body, yet in my flesh shall I see God."*[153]

Teachings

The Torah teaches and speaks of many topics, some of which are mentioned elsewhere in this summary. A partial list includes the following:

Abraham, covenant
Adam, Eve
Angels
Apostasy
ark of covenant
atonement, blood
business, ethics
children, teach
Commandments
Covenant
Creation
Dreams
employer, employees
Faith
false gods
father, honor, and mother
fear, God

feast, Passover
feast, tabernacles
feast, unleavened bread
Flood
Forgiveness
Garden of Eden
Geneology
God, appearance, bodily features
God, merciful, requirements
God, name of
God, nature of
God, power of
gold plates
Humility
Israel, camp
Israel, gathering and return of
Israel, in Egypt
Israel, in wilderness
Israel, scatter
Jacob, son of Isaac
Jesus Christ, symbol of
Joseph, brothers
Joseph, dream
Joseph, reunion with family
Joshua
Jubilee
Judah
judgment, civil
land, inheritance
latter-days

law, of Moses
Leah
Levites
Lot
love, God
Manasseh, son of Jacob
Marriage
marriage, plural
marriage, unity
medical, leprosy
mercy, obtaining
Messiah
Messiah, prophecy of
Moses
mount…mountain
Murder
Murmuring
nations, destruction
necessities, miracle providing
Noah, son of Lamech
Noah's Ark
Obedience
obedience, sacrifice, better than
parenting, teaching
Patience
patriarchal order
peculiar people
poor, give to
Pray
Priestcraft

priesthood leaders, sustaining and respecting
Priesthood, Aaronic or Levitical
Priesthood, Melchizedek, ancient Israel
Prophets
Prosperity
Rebel
Remember
repentance, how
revelation, obtaining
Sabbath, keeping holy
sacrifice, of children, evil
sacrifice, unauthorized
Sarah
scriptures, use of
sexual sin
signs, purpose
Sodom and Gomorrah
Tabernacle
Tithing
trial, kinds of
trial, responding to
trust, God
Urim and Thummim
Vengeance
Vow
War
widow, fatherless
witnesses, false
witnesses, law of
Women

word of wisdom, ancient, prohibited
Worship

The Nevi'im and Ketuvim also reference most of these same topics. In addition, they give some added insight into other topics, some of which are here listed:

Abomination
Adam-ondi-Ahman
agency, choose
anger (angry)
Animals
Babylon
Book of Mormon
chariots, prophecy, cut off
chastisement, bear
children, parents
cities, destroyed
Contention
contention, pride causes
counsel, not the Lord
Daniel, visions
David
death, spiritual
death, temporal
Desire
earth, Christ's second coming
Egypt
Elisha
Esther
evil, return good

fast, power of
Father, Heavenly, offspring, children
fear, not
Gentiles
God, anger
God, forgiving
God, knowledge
God, seek for
government, leaders
gratitude, to God
happiness, personal
healing, faith to be healed
heart, change
heart, hard
Integrity
Israel and Judah
Jeremiah
Jerusalem, at war
Jerusalem, chosen
Jerusalem, defend
Jerusalem, destruction
Jerusalem, inhabitants
Jerusalem, temple
Jerusalem, wall
John the Baptist, prophecy of
Jonah
Jonathan
judgment, how, by works
king, Israel
king, Judah

king, Zedekiah
knowledge, how obtained, by revelation
Lehi, place
lost ten tribes
love, brotherly
lust, for women
man, dominion of
mercy, power of
Messiah, Atonement
Messiah, betrayal to death
Messiah, betrayal to death, wounds
Messiah, body, marks
Messiah, come unto
Messiah, King
Messiah, names of
Messiah, prophecy of, (1) mortal coming
Messiah, prophecy of, (2) glorious coming
Messiah, recognition as the Messiah
Messiah, second coming
Messiah, worship
Michael
Millenium, Jesus Christ
Millenium, peace
missionary service
Nebuchadnezzar
New Jerusalem
opposition, overcoming
parenting, correcting
Peace
pondering and meditation

praise, God
pray, for deliverance
pray, how
premortal life
pride, characteristics of
pride, consequence of
priesthood leaders, sustaining and respecting
priesthood, false
prophets, following and honoring
prophets, revelation to
prophets, warning
protection, safety, dwell in
Purity
repentance, necessary
restore, for evil
restore, for good
Resurrection
revelation, dreams and visions
rich and riches
Righteous
salvation, from sins, conditions for
Samson
Samuel
Saul
seek, for Lord
Seer
self discipline
servant and service
sexual sin, temptation
Shepherd

sin, pain and unhappiness
sing, praises
slavery, Israel
Solomon
Speaking
spirit world, spirit prison
sun, darkened
teach, how
Teachable
Temple
temple, setting
temple, use
Thoughts
trial, causes
trial, purpose and necessity of
vision (heavenly view)
wait upon the Lord, blessings
war, ancient Israel
wicked, characteristics of, unhappy
wicked, destruction of
wisdom, source, from God
works, judged of, deeds
Zion

Miracles

Many miracles are spoken of in the Torah, as well as the Nevi'im and Ketuvim. These include, but are not limited to,

1. God's creation of the earth and placing Adam and Eve in the Garden of Eden;[154]
2. Noah's building of and entering the ark;[155]

3. Rescuing of Lot from Sodom and Gomorrah;[156]
4. Abraham and Sarah conceiving and giving birth to Isaac;[157]
5. Joseph's interpretation of Pharaoh's dreams and the preservation of Israel during a famine;[158]
6. Plagues announced by Moses upon the Egyptians;[159]
7. The passing over of an angel upon the houses of Israel if they marked their posts with the blood of the Passover lamb;[160]
8. The parting of the Red Sea as the Israelites crossed fleeing from the Egyptians;[161]
9. The pillar of fire delaying the Egyptians pursuit of the Israelites into the Red Sea;[162]
10. The closing of the Red Sea upon the armies of the Egyptians;[163]
11. God sending the plague which killed 14,700 in the matter of the rebellious Korah;[164]
12. Moses receiving the Ten commandments;[165]
13. Moses, Aaron, Nadab and Abihu and seventy elders seeing the God of Israel;[166]
14. The healing of Israel if they would have faith to look upon the serpent fastened to a pole;[167]
15. The sun standing still;[168]
16. The sun turning back 10 degrees (40 minutes);[169]
17. Jordan River waters stopping as the priests of Joshua crossed;[170]
18. Elijah's prayer and the destruction of Baal's prophets;[171]
19. Healing of Naaman as he washed in the river Jordan seven times;[172]
20. Esther's dangerous approach to king Ahasuerus, and the saving of the Jews;[173]
21. The swimming of an ax head in water;[174]
22. The sudden fleeing of the Syrian hosts in the twilight;[175]
23. The destruction of 185,000 Asyrian soldiers;[176]
24. The falling down of Jericho's walls;[177]
25. The widow's barrel of meal and cruise of oil not failing as Elijah promised;[178]

26. Bringing back to life the widow's son;[179]
27. David's slaying of Goliath;[180]
28. Solomon's wisdom in discerning who was the true mother of the contested baby;[181]
29. Hannah conceiving a son;[182]
30. Daniel's interpretation of Nebuchadnezzar's dream;[183]
31. Daniel, Shadrach, Meshack, and Abednego protected from fiery furnace;[184]
32. Daniel protected from den of lions;[185]
33. God sending manna to feed Israel in the wilderness;[186]
34. Moses striking the stone and water coming forth;[187]
35. Elijah ascending to heaven;[188]
36. God appearing unto Solomon;[189] and,
37. Jonah being saved from the whale.[190]

Establishment of Church

The Torah does not use the word "church." Instead, however, it refers to congregations and to a religious body, "Israel."

Within these congregations there are recognized priesthood leaders, such as Moses[191], Joshua[192], and Elijah[193].

Within the religious body there was a well-established priesthood order. When this order was violated, even with unauthorized help, it met with the displeasure of God.[194]

It is interesting to note that some teach that Moses,[195] Elijah,[196] and Elias[197] have returned to earth to transfer priesthood authority to modern prophets.

Temples

The Torah, Nevi'im, and Ketuvim speak of the following tabernacles and temples:

1. The tabernacle of Israel in the wilderness;[198]

2. The temple of Solomon;[199]
3. A temple to be built in the last days;[200] and,
4. That God would suddenly come to His temple.[201]

A tabernacle or temple is a place for the presence of God,[202] and refuge.[203]

Gathering of Israel

The Torah, Nevi'im, and Ketuvim speak of a "scattering" of Israel,[204] and also a "gathering"[205] of Israel.

This gathering includes a return to promised lands of Israel.[206]

In addition to a physical gathering, others have described this gathering as a spiritual one[207] where covenants are again made with God,[208] including the covenants of baptism.[209]

Still others suggest that particular promises to "Israel" who will be gathered include those of any genealogical ancestry so long as they will make required covenants with God,[210] and that those of genealogical descent from Jacob, renamed Israel, who refuse making and keeping the covenants are not included in the "Israel"[211] which was promised certain latter-day gathering blessings. Thus, there are those who believe that the promised blessings to Israel are dispensed on purely a racial basis, while others believe that the promised blessings to Israel are dispensed on a covenantal basis, and include those of any racial ancestry if they choose to yield and make and keep such covenants with God.

In summary, "Israel", for some, is understood on purely an ancestral basis alone, while to others "Israel" is understood on a "faith in" and "covenant with" God basis, inclusive of those of all different ancestries.

To the former believers the "gathering of Israel" references solely the return of literal descendants of Jacob to lands of inheritance promised by God. To the latter believers the "gathering of Israel" references the spreading of God's word throughout the earth and a growing movement of people who freely make and keep covenants with God.

Commandments

The Torah, Nevi'im and Ketuvim encompass many commandments. Some of these include the following:

- **Ten Commandments**

    1. Thou shalt have no other gods before me.[212]
    2. Thou shalt not make unto thee any graven image, or any likeness of any thing that is in heaven above, or that is in the earth beneath, or that is in the water under the earth.[213]

Thou shalt not bow down thyself to them, nor serve them: for I the LORD thy God am a jealous God, visiting the iniquity of the fathers upon the children unto the third and fourth generation of them that hate me;[214] And shewing mercy unto thousands of them that love me, and keep my commandments.

    3. Thou shalt not take the name of the LORD thy God in vain; for the LORD will not hold him guiltless that taketh his name in vain.[215]
    4. Remember the sabbath day, to keep it holy.[216]

    Six days shalt thou labour, and do all thy work:[217]
    But the seventh day is the sabbath of the LORD thy God: in it thou shalt not do any work, thou, nor thy son, nor thy daughter, thy manservant, nor thy maidservant, nor thy cattle, nor thy stranger that is within thy gates:[218]
    For in six days the LORD made heaven and earth, the sea, and all that in them is, and rested the seventh day: wherefore the LORD blessed the sabbath day, and hallowed it.

    5. Honour thy father and thy mother: that thy days may be long upon the land which the LORD thy God giveth thee.[219]

6. Thou shalt not kill.[220]
7. Thou shalt not commit adultery.[221]
8. Thou shalt not steal.[222]
9. Thou shalt not bear false witness against thy neighbour.[223]
10. Thou shalt not covet thy neighbour's house, thou shalt not covet thy neighbour's wife, nor his manservant, nor his maidservant, nor his ox, nor his ass, nor any thing that is thy neighbour's.[224]

The Law of Moses contains many other commandments / directions for Ancient Israel, and relate to the following:

11. If a woman hides adultery;[225]
12. If a man strives with a woman and causes her to lose her unborn;[226]
13. If a man causes death of another, under a variety of circumstances and motives;[227]
14. If a man smiteth his father or mother;[228]
15. If a man curse his father or mother;[229]
16. If a man lieth with a beast;[230]
17. If a man borrow;[231]
18. Charging excessive interest, or usury, to the poor;[232]
19. Afflicting any widow or fatherless child;[233]
20. Letting the land rest in the seventh year;[234]
21. Giving the firstborn to God;[235]
22. Marrying a maid who was enticed and with whom a man lay;[236]
23. Not cursing the ruler of any people;[237]
24. Imposing judgment of an "eye for an eye";[238]
25. Kidnapping a man;[239]
26. Providing for a second wife;[240]
27. Restitution for an ox falling into an open, uncovered pit;[241]
28. Restitution or death for an ox causing injury or death;[242]
29. Stealing an ox;[243]
30. Returning an enemy's ox if found;[244]
31. Sacrificing unto any God, except the Lord;[245]
32. Oppressing a stranger;[246]

33. Restoring double that which was stolen;[247]
34. Fearing God; and,[248]
35. Not suffering a witch to live.[249]
36. In addition, the Torah contains multiple passages relating to various dietary rules, including not eating that which (a) dieth of itself,[250] (b) has a cloven hoof,[251] (c) is from swine,[252] or (d) is an eagle,[253] hawk,[254] or swan.[255] Many other rules and restrictions apply, including that a kid shall not be seethed (boiled) in its mother's milk.[256]
37. The Torah also contains many directions relating to the Tabernacle and the offering of sacrifices.

Sacrifice

The Torah, Nevi'im and Ketuvim speak extensively of sacrificing to God.[257]

One of the premier accounts of sacrifice is Abraham's willingness to sacrifice his only son, Isaac.[258] In doing so, Abraham "rose up early"[259] to start upon the journey, humbly bound his beloved son upon the place of sacrifice, and even raised his hand in the death-stroke upon his son.[260] At the last moment, he was stopped by an angel who commanded him not to lay his hand upon the lad.[261]

But Abraham had shown God his willingness to love God even above his own family and self-interests.[262] Abraham was given great blessings and promises because of his faithfulness.[263]

Other religious texts suggest that this experience taught Abraham something of the sacrifice God the Father would make in sacrificing His Beloved Son, Jesus Christ.[264]

The account teaches that man should withhold nothing from God, but be willing to sacrifice all.

Many animal sacrifices were part of the Mosaic law and were also included in the sacrifices made in the Tabernacle[265] and Solomon's temple.[266]

Features of these sacrifices include that they would,

1) be part of the forgiving of sin;[267]
2) must be made of an animal without blemish;[268] and,
3) be authorized and performed by God and His priesthood servants.[269]

In addition, these texts indicate that mankind should sacrifice a broken heart and a contrite spirit.[270]

Other texts indicate that this sacrifice of a broken heart and a contrite spirit is a necessary part in repenting and seeking for a forgiveness of sin.[271]

CHAPTER 2

Shrimad Bhagavad Gita

The Shrimad Bhagavad Gita

The Bhagavad Gita tells of an extensive conversation between the Supreme Lord Krishna and Arjun.

Krishna relays teachings on many topics to Arjun, including:

I. The nature and identity of Krishna, as well as Krishna's relationship to other gods, such as Brahman;
II. The three modes of goodness, passion, and ignorance;
III. The importance of being detached from the fruits of one's actions;
IV. The several yog, or alternate pathways, back to Krishna's abode, including the
   a) Yog of action, sacrifice, and service;
   b) Yog of renunciation and knowledge;
   c) Yog of devotion; and,
   d) Yog of meditation.
V. The importance of performing one's natural occupation—whether Brahmins, Kshatriyas, Vaishyas, or Shudras;
VI. Doer. The Bhagavad Gita gives an explanation of who the "doer" is inside us, and who is rewarded or punished based upon that doing; and,
VII. Reincarnation, a temporary spirit world, and hell.

I. Nature and Identity of Krishna

The Bhagavad Gita says so much about Krishna, no adequate summary can be provided. Nevertheless, some important passages include:

"Those who know Me as unborn and beginningless, and as the Supreme Lord of the universe, they among mortals are free from illusion and released from all evils."[1]

"Being freed from attachment, fear, and anger, becoming fully absorbed in me, and taking refuge in me, many persons in the past

became purified by knowledge of me, and thus they attained my divine love."²

"Although He is all-pervading and all living beings are situated in Him, yet He can be known only through devotion."³

"One who departs from the body while remembering Me, the Supreme Personality, and chanting the syllable Om, will attain the supreme goal."⁴

"But on attaining My Abode, O son of Kunti, there is no further rebirth."⁵

"I am the basis of the formless Brahman, the immortal and imperishable, of eternal dharma, and of unending divine bliss."⁶

"Know that I am like the brilliance of the sun that illuminates the entire solar system."⁷

"But those who worship the formless aspect of the Absolute Truth—the imperishable, the indefinable, the unmanifest, the all-pervading, the unthinkable, the unchanging, the eternal, and the immoveable—by restraining their senses and being even-minded everywhere, such persons, engaged in the welfare of all beings, also attain Me."⁸

"Those who perform all their duties for My sake, who depend upon Me and are devoted to Me, who are free from attachment, and are without malice toward all beings, such devotees certainly come to Me."⁹

"The Supreme Lord dwells in the hearts of all living beings, O Arjun."¹⁰

"You are the Father of the entire universe, of all moving and non-moving beings. You are the most deserving of worship and the Supreme Spiritual Master."¹¹

"All living beings dwell in Me, but I do not dwell in them."¹²

"I see Your infinite form in every direction, with countless arms, stomachs, faces, and eyes."¹³

"You are Vāyu (god of wind), Yamraj (god of death), Agni (god of fire), Varuṇ (god of water), and Chandra (moon-god)."¹⁴

"You are the primeval God and the original Divine Personality."¹⁵

"Amongst purifiers, I am the wind, and amongst wielders of weapons, I am Lord Ram. Of water creatures, I am the crocodile, and of flowing rivers, I am the Ganges."[16]

"Amongst sciences I am the science of spirituality, and in debates I am the logical conclusion."[17]

"Amongst secrets I am silence, and in the wise I am their wisdom."[18]

"Permeating the earth, I nourish all living beings with My energy."[19]

"Both you and I have had many births, O Arjun."[20]

"From Me alone arises…control over the senses and mind, joy and sorrow, birth and death, fear and courage, non-violence, equanimity, contentment, austerity, charity, fame, and infamy."[21]

II. Three Modes of Material Nature

The Bhagavad Gita speaks of the material nature of man, sometimes called gunas. It identifies three "modes" of material nature—the mode of goodness, the mode of passion, and the mode of ignorance.

It is not clear whether these modes are entirely the consequence of one's birth, or whether they also are the result of one's choices during life.

How much of one's material nature comes with them at the time of birth, and how much is developed through one's own choices during life?

- **Material Mode comes At Birth**

Whether one has a material nature already at the time of birth begs the question whether one's previous material nature comes with them following death.

The Bhagavad Gita states that the mind and senses of an individual do continue with its soul after death:

> *"As the air carries fragrance from place to place, so does the embodied soul carry the mind and senses with it, when it leaves an old body and enters a new one."*[22]

Is this also true for the material natures? Typically, the Bhagavad Gita speaks of the mind and senses as independent of the three gunas, perhaps suggesting that the mind and senses in a reincarnated body do not come with their prior gunas.

On the other hand, the existence at the time of death of one of these three modes—for example, goodness or ignorance—is the cause for an individual to enter the pure abodes of the learned, or to be reincarnated as an animal. The question remains if that goodness (sattva) or ignorance causing the next life station, is in fact left behind and not part of the new abode, or the new animal.

> *"Those who die with predominance of sattva reach the pure abodes of the learned"*;[23] and
>
> *"[T]hose dying in the mode of ignorance take birth in the animal kingdom."*[24]

- **Material Mode caused by Life's Choices**

Or, alternatively, it may indicate that the cause of such next life station, is the result of one's prior life's choices, which a reincarnated being is encouraged to then improve upon.

There are multiple passages encouraging a being to "fix your mind steadily on Me (Krishna)",[25] "practice remembering Me",[26] "constantly restrain the mind from worldly affairs",[27] try to work for Krishna, control one's mind and senses, discard all cravings of the senses and all selfish desires. All these passages imply a capacity to make a choice and improve one's mode.

- **Mode of Goodness (Sattva)**

When is action in accordance with the "mode of goodness"? The Bhagavad Gita states that it is when:

1. free from attachment and aversion;[28]
2. in accordance with scriptures;[29]
3. the performer is endowed with enthusiasm and determination;[30]
4. the performer is free from egotism and attachment;[31]
5. the performer is equipoised in success and failure;[32]
6. without desire for rewards;[33] and,
7. which are undertaken out of a sense of duty and one relinquishes attachment to any reward.[34]

In addition to the above kinds of actions, the mode of goodness includes:

- A. Austerity without yearning for material rewards;[35]
- B. Charity given to worthy persons simply because it is right;[36]
- C. Charity given without consideration of return and in the proper time and place;[37]
- D. Determination and steadfast willpower developed through Yog;[38]
- E. An intellect when it understands what is duty and non-duty;[39]
- F. An intellect when it understands what is proper and improper action;[40]
- G. An intellect when it understands what is to be feared;[41]
- H. Knowledge that there is one undivided imperishable reality in diverse beings;[42] and,
- I. Not seeking to avoid disagreeable work nor seek for agreeable work.[43]

- **Mode of Passion**

The mode of passion is described by the Bhagavad Gita as follows:

> "Action that is prompted by selfish desire, enacted with pride, and full of stress, is in the nature of passion."[44]
>
> "Action that is prompted by selfish desire, enacted with pride, and full of stress, is in the nature of passion."[45]
>
> "The performer is considered in the mode of passion when he or she craves the fruits of the work, is covetous, violent-natured, impure, and moved by joy and sorrow."[46]

- **Mode of Ignorance**

The Bhagavad Gita describes the mode of ignorance actions in several ways:

> "A performer in the mode of ignorance is one who is undisciplined, vulgar, stubborn, deceitful, slothful, despondent, and a procrastinator."[47]
>
> "That action is declared to be in the mode of ignorance, which is begun out of delusion, without thought to one's own ability, and disregarding consequences, loss, and injury to others."[48]

The mode of ignorance and austerity, charity, and determination are described as follows:

> "Austerity that is performed by those with confused notions, and which involves torturing the self or harming others, is described to be in the mode of ignorance."[49]
>
> "And that charity, which is given at the wrong place and wrong time to unworthy persons, without showing respect, or with contempt, is held to be of the nature of nescience."[50]
>
> "That unintelligent resolve is said to be determination in the mode of ignorance, in which one does not give up dreaming, fearing, grieving, despair, and conceit."[51]

Happiness, intellect, knowledge and the mode of ignorance are described as follows:

> *"That happiness which covers the nature of the self from beginning to end, and which is derived from sleep, indolence, and negligence, is said to be in the mode of ignorance."*[52]
>
> *"That intellect which is shrouded in darkness, imagining irreligion to be religion, and perceiving untruth to be the truth, is of the nature of ignorance, O Parth."*[53]
>
> *"That knowledge is said to be in the mode of ignorance where one is engrossed in a fragmental concept as if it encompasses the whole, and which is neither grounded in reason nor based on the truth."*[54]

Finally, the Bhagavad Gita states that the renunciation of prescribed duties is in the mode of ignorance:

> *"Such deluded renunciation is said to be in the mode of ignorance."*[55]

III. Importance of Being Detached

Being or becoming detached is important in the Bhagavad Gita. Specifically, a person is to become detached from the fruits of one's actions.

> *"Those, who are alike to friend and foe, equipoised in honor and dishonor, cold and heat, joy and sorrow, and are free from all unfavorable association; those who take praise and reproach alike, who are given to silent contemplation, content with what comes their way, without attachment to the place of residence, whose intellect is firmly fixed in Me, and who are full of devotion to Me, such persons are very dear to Me."*[56]

- **Free from Selfishness**

Becoming free from selfishness is important. Accordingly, the Bhagavad Gita explains, one should,

> *"discard…all selfish desires and cravings of the senses that torment the mind, and become[ ] satisfied in the realization of the self."*[57]

Further,

> "[t]hose who are indifferent to worldly gains, externally and internally pure, skillful, without cares, untroubled, and free from selfishness in all undertakings, such devotees of Mine are very dear to Me."[58]

- ## Senses and Desires

The Bhagavad Gita thus speaks both of the senses and desires of a person, as well as the sense objects.

> "When one is neither attached to sense objects nor to actions, such a person is said to be elevated in the science of Yog, having renounced all desires for the fruits of actions."[59]

> "[T]he contact between the senses and the sense objects gives rise to fleeting perceptions of happiness and distress."[60]

It is the selfish desires and cravings of the senses that one should renounce. It is not to say that one should avoid all actions and its fruits, but that one should avoid the selfish desire of the fruits of those actions, which lead to "fleeting perceptions" of happiness.

- ## Happiness and Peace

A key qualifier to this doctrine is that mankind can seek to be at peace and happy. True peace and happiness—not fleeting happiness—is not at the expense of others, and not selfish. Indeed, the sought-after abode of Krishna is a place of love, and peace comes by uniting the mind with God.

> "Being freed from attachment, fear, and anger, becoming fully absorbed in me, and taking refuge in me, many persons in the past became purified by knowledge of me, and thus they attained my divine love."[61]

> "For one who never unites the mind with God there is no peace; and how can one who lacks peace be happy?"[62]

IV. Pathways Back to Krishna

The following describe various pathways back to Krishna, receiving liberation, spiritual consciousness, and peace.

While described separately, these pathways may have some overlapping and not be mutually exclusive of each other.

▪ Action, Sacrifice, and Service

Regarding karma, or action, sacrifice and service, the Bhagavad Gita states:

"But those who dedicate all their actions to Me...worshiping Me and meditating on Me with exclusive devotion...their consciousness is united with Me."[63]

"[W]hen one discards all selfish desires and cravings of the senses that torment the mind, and becomes satisfied in the realization of the self, such a person is said to be transcendentally situated."[64]

"Since they perform all actions as a sacrifice (to God), they are freed from all karmic reactions."[65]

"Those who serve Me with unalloyed devotion rise above the three modes of material nature and come to the level of the Brahman."[66]

▪ Renunciation and Knowledge

Regarding renunciation and knowledge the Bhagavad Gita states:

"[C]an there be a better way of living other than renouncing the world and its things and remaining detached from them?"[67]

"One should stay amidst the world, but pursue Brahman through detachment and performance of ones ordained duties."[68]

"Through such transcendental knowledge, they quickly attain everlasting supreme peace."[69]

"Those who are not attached to external sense pleasures realize divine bliss in the self."[70]

> "Being freed from attachment, fear, and anger, becoming fully absorbed in me, and taking refuge in me, many persons in the past became purified by knowledge of me, and thus they attained my divine love."[71]

> "[B]eyond the dualities of pleasure and pain, such liberated personalities attain My eternal Abode."[72]

> "I shall now reveal to you that which ought to be known, and by knowing which, one attains immortality. It is the beginningless Brahman, which lies beyond existence and non-existence."[73]

> "[N]othing as purifying as divine knowledge."[74]

> "Through such transcendental knowledge, they quickly attain everlasting supreme peace."[75]

- ## Devotion, Remembering, and Worshipping

Regarding devotion, remembering, and worshipping, the Bhagavad Gita states:

> "They are ever-content, steadily united with Me in devotion, self-controlled, of firm resolve, and dedicated to Me in mind and intellect."[76]

> "With practice, O Parth, when you constantly engage the mind in remembering Me, the Supreme Divine Personality, without deviating, you will certainly attain Me."[77]

> "One who departs from the body while remembering Me, the Supreme Personality, and chanting the syllable Om, will attain the supreme goal."[78]

> "Those who relinquish the body while remembering Me at the moment of death will come to Me. There is certainly no doubt about this."[79]

> "There are those who always think of Me and engage in exclusive devotion to Me."[80]

> "Others, engaging in the yajña of cultivating knowledge, worship Me by many methods."[81]

- **Meditation**

Several Bhagavad Gita passages on meditation include:

> "To the soul who is aspiring for perfection in Yog, work without attachment is said to be the means; to the sage who is already elevated in Yog, tranquility in meditation is said to be the means."[82]

> "Seated firmly on it, the yogi should strive to purify the mind by focusing it in meditation with one pointed concentration, controlling all thoughts and activities."[83]

> "Better than meditation is renunciation of the fruits of actions, for peace immediately follows such renunciation."[84]

V. Performing One's Natural Occupation

> "The duties of the Brahmins, Kshatriyas, Vaishyas, and Shudras—are distributed according to their qualities, in accordance with their guṇas."[85]

The three material natures, or gunas, are goodness, passion, and ignorance.

> Brahmins: "Tranquility, restraint, austerity, purity, patience, integrity, knowledge, wisdom, and belief in a hereafter—these are the intrinsic qualities of work for Brahmins."[86]

> Kshatriyas: "Valor, strength, fortitude, skill in weaponry, resolve never to retreat from battle, large-heartedness in charity, and leadership abilities, these are the natural qualities of work for Kshatriyas."[87]

> Vaishyas: "Agriculture, dairy farming, and commerce are the natural works for those with the qualities of Vaishyas."[88]

> Shudras: "Serving through work is the natural duty for those with the qualities of Shudras."[89]

> Even if one finds this work somewhat unsuitable, he or she should not shirk away from it:

> "One should not abandon duties born of one's nature, even if one sees defects in them, O son of Kunti."[90]
>
> By performing the work of one's natural occupation, he or she is protected from sin, worships the Creator, and "easily attains perfection."[91]
>
> "By doing one's innate duties, a person does not incur sin."[92]
>
> "By performing one's natural occupation, one worships the Creator from whom all living entities have come into being, and by whom the whole universe is pervaded."[93]
>
> "By such performance of work, a person easily attains perfection."[94]

VI. Doer

One of the important elements of the Bhagavad Gita is its discussion of the "doer"—who or what it is that makes our decisions.

The full intertwining of concepts is not set forth, but some pieces include the following:

1) Krishna Himself, as the Supreme Lord present in every person "directs our wanderings."[95] The Bhagavad Gita states:

   > "According to their karmas, He directs the wanderings of the souls, who are seated on a machine made of material energy."[96]

2) Other passages highlight this material energy, or the material nature or gunas of "goodness, passion, and ignorance" as responsible for our choices:

   > "They alone truly see who understand that all actions (of the body) are performed by material nature, while the embodied soul actually does nothing."[97]

3) In addition to this clear pronunciation that the "soul actually does nothing",[98] still other passages emphasize that the soul is not the doer:

> "[I]n ignorance, the soul, deluded by false identification with the body, thinks itself to be the doer."[99]

4) The individual soul, however, is clearly stated to be the part of oneself responsible for happiness:

> "In the matter of creation, the material energy is responsible for cause and effect; in the matter of experiencing happiness and distress, the individual soul is declared responsible."[100]

5) It should be noted, as referenced earlier, that the individual soul upon death of the body takes the mind and senses with it:

> "As the air carries fragrance from place to place, so does the embodied soul carry the mind and senses with it, when it leaves an old body and enters a new one."[101]

6) Finally, the Bhagavad Gita speaks of self-control this way:

> "The embodied beings who are self-controlled and detached reside happily in the city of nine gates, free from thinking they are the doers or the cause of anything."[102]

7) In addition, the Bhagavad Gita speaks of one's willpower:

> "The steadfast willpower that is developed through Yog, and which sustains the activities of the mind, the life-airs, and the senses, O Parth, is said to be determination in the mode of goodness."[103]

8) Upon death, with the body left behind, and the soul rewarded or punished together with the mind and senses, the question remains whether the soul is being judged even if it does not make any choices—if the decisions were made exclusively by the now dead body. As highlighted earlier, while it may be subject to the temptations of the material man, or the gunas, "the individual soul is declared responsible" in the "matter of experiencing happiness."[104] If the soul is responsible for happiness, then the

question exists whether it is that part of self which exercises "self-control"[105] and exerts "willpower."[106]

VII. Reincarnation

The Bhagavad Gita states that upon death a person experiences one of three results: (a) they are immediately reincarnated into another body, (b) they go to a world where they enjoy and use up the merits of their life, and then are reincarnated, or (c) they go to Krishna's abode never to be reincarnated again.

The Bhagavad Gita states that

> *"those dying in the mode of ignorance take birth in the animal kingdom",*[107]
>
> *"[t]hose who die with prevalence of the mode of passion are born among people driven by work",*[108] *and*
>
> *"[t]hose whose intellect is fixed in God, who are wholly absorbed in God, with firm faith in Him as the supreme goal, such persons quickly reach the state from which there is no return, their sins having been dispelled by the light of knowledge."*[109]

- ## Going to Ancestors

It also states that "worshippers of the ancestors go to the ancestors."[110] The exact meaning of this is not set forth since most ancestors will have already been reincarnated in either animal or human form.

- ## Temporary Spirit World

For some, reincarnation is not immediate, but comes only after the soul goes to the "abode of Indra."[111] There they can enjoy the merits of their life, and once those merits are used up are then reincarnated.

The Bhagavad Gita explains this concept this way:

> *"By virtue of their pious deeds, they go to the abode of Indra, the king of heaven, and enjoy the pleasures of the celestial gods",*[112] *and,*

"When they have enjoyed the vast pleasures of heaven, the stock of their merits being exhausted, they return to the earthly plane."[113]

- **Hell**

A "hell" is spoken of at least twice in the Bhagavad Gita. Exactly how it operates in conjunction with one's reincarnation is not fully specified. One option may be that it stands in opposition to the "abode of Indra", and is also a temporary location prior to reincarnation.

Here are the two passages,

"I have heard from the learned that those who destroy family traditions dwell in hell for an indefinite period of time."[114]

"Possessed and led astray by such imaginings, enveloped in a mesh of delusion, and addicted to the gratification of sensuous pleasures, they descend to the murkiest hell."[115]

VIII. Supreme Goal

Those who have Krishna as the Supreme Goal and are successful in worshiping and meditating on Him with exclusive devotion are liberated from the cycle of birth and death and have their consciousness united with Krishna.

The Bhagavad Gita explains this result this way,

"But those who dedicate all their actions to Me, regarding Me as the Supreme goal, worshiping Me and meditating on Me with exclusive devotion, O Parth, I swiftly deliver them from the ocean of birth and death, for their consciousness is united with Me."[116]

CHAPTER 3

The Book of Mormon: Another Testament of Jesus Christ

The Book of Mormon: Another Testament of Jesus Christ

The Book of Mormon: Another Testament of Jesus Christ is a companion witness with the Torah, Nevi'im and Ketuvim, and also the New Testament.

The Jewish prophets prophesied of a Messiah who would come to Zion,[1] a Prince of Peace[2] who would be born and come forth from Bethlehem,[3] with the government upon His shoulders.[4]

The Book of Mormon likewise prophesies of the Messiah,[5] and proclaims that this Savior would be raised up among the Jews.[6] It states that all mankind were in a lost and fallen state, and ever would be save they should rely on this Redeemer.[7]

The Book of Mormon records the words and teachings of Jewish prophets, who left Jerusalem around 600 B.C.[8]

The New Testament witnesses that this prophesied Messiah came[9] and was born in a manger as Jesus Christ.[10] It speaks of His teachings,[11] gospel,[12] and atonement[13] that he suffered for the sins of all mankind.[14] It also speaks of His resurrection[15] when in three days His spirit came again into His body.[16]

The Book of Mormon, as its subtitle indicates, is "Another Testament of Jesus Christ." It also tells of remarkable solar events surrounding the birth of Jesus Christ which caused the night to be as bright as during the day.[17] It proclaims His teachings,[18] gospel,[19] and atonement,[20] and that He suffered for the sins of all mankind.[21] It also teaches of the resurrection of Jesus Christ and all mankind.[22] Then, it relates the stunning account of the appearance of the resurrected Jesus Christ Himself,[23] descending from the heavens to a people gathered at a temple.[24]

Jesus Christ proclaimed that He was the prophesied One,[25] and invited all to come and feel the print marks in His hands and feet[26] that they might all know that He truly was the Son of God who had been slain for the sins of the world.[27]

The Book of Mormon itself speaks to several important topics, including the following.

Jesus Christ

The Book of Mormon states that Jesus Christ is the Son of God.[28] It joins the New Testament in witnessing that Jesus Christ is the long-awaited Messiah.[29]

It speaks of His birth, describing the fulfillment of a prophecy[30] that when the Christ-child should be born, that there would be a day, and a night, and a day, as though they were one day.[31]

It then tells of an account, over thirty years later, when the people are gathered at a temple.[32] Great destructive storms and earthquakes had racked the earth because of the death of Jesus Christ.[33] Sometime thereafter, they heard a voice from heaven, saying, "This is My Beloved Son, Hear Him."[34]

They then saw a Man descending out of heaven in a white robe.[35] He came and stood in the midst of them, and said, "I am Jesus Christ, whom the prophets testified shall come into the world."[36]

He then invited all there to "[a]rise and come forth unto me, that ye may thrust your hands into my side, and also that ye may feel the prints of the nails in my hands and in my feet, that ye may know that I am the God of Israel, and the God of the whole earth, and have been slain for the sins of the world."[37]

Throughout the Book of Mormon there were various groups of believers and followers of the Messiah,[38] led by prophets,[39] who lived the law of Moses,[40] and the additional teachings Jesus Christ taught when He came.[41]

The name Jesus Christ or Lord is found in the Book of Mormon over 1,000 times.

Prophecies of Messiah's First Coming

The Book of Mormon, like the Torah, Nevi'im, and Ketuvim, prophesies that a Messiah shall come.[42] The Book begins in Jerusalem during the reign of king Zedekiah, approximately 600 B.C.[43] and continues until after 400 A.D.[44]

One prophet, named Lehi, spoke of the coming Messiah this way:

"Wherefore, redemption cometh in and through the Holy Messiah; for he is full of grace and truth.

"Behold, he offereth himself a sacrifice for sin, to answer the ends of the law, unto all those who have a broken heart and a contrite spirit; and unto none else can the ends of the law be answered.

"Wherefore, how great the importance to make these things known unto the inhabitants of the earth, that they may know that there is no flesh that can dwell in the presence of God, save it be through the merits, and mercy, and grace of the Holy Messiah, who layeth down his life according to the flesh, and taketh it again by the power of the Spirit, that he may bring to pass the resurrection of the dead, being the first that should rise."[45]

Later, another Book of Mormon prophet, named Abinadi, who reminded and taught the people from the words of Moses and Isaiah said:

"For behold, did not Moses prophesy unto them concerning the coming of the Messiah, and that God should redeem his people? Yea, and even all the prophets who have prophesied ever since the world began—have they not spoken more or less concerning these things?

> "Have they not said that God himself should come down among the children of men, and take upon him the form of man, and go forth in mighty power upon the face of the earth?
>
> "Yea, and have they not said also that he should bring to pass the resurrection of the dead, and that he, himself should be oppressed and afflicted?"[46]

Fulfillment of Prophecies of Messiah's First Coming

Like the New Testament, the Book of Mormon witnesses that Jesus Christ was and is the promised Messiah, the Son of God.[47]

Although prophesied by Book of Mormon prophets, the Book itself does not tell the day-by-day account of Jesus Christ's teachings and miracles—because that was a continent away. A prophet named Benjamin said:

> "For, behold, the time cometh, and is not far distant, that with power, the Lord Omnipotent who reigneth, who was, and is from all eternity to all eternity, shall come down from heaven among the children of men, and shall dwell in a tabernacle of clay, and shall go forth amongst men, working mighty miracles, such as healing the sick, raising the dead, causing the lame to walk, the blind to receive their sight, and the deaf to hear, and curing all manner of diseases....
>
> "And lo, he shall suffer temptations, and pain of body, hunger, thirst, and fatigue, even more than man can suffer, except it be unto death; for behold, blood cometh from every pore, so great shall be his anguish for the wickedness and the abominations of his people."[48]

The sign of Jesus Christ's birth was a spectacular event across the oceans in America. A prophet named Samuel had said that God would give a sign of the Messiah's birth—that a day, a night, and a day should all be bright as though it were one day.[49]

Christian believers prayerfully awaited such a day, but it did not come.[50] Finally, the government issued an order that on a day certain all such believers should be slain, if the sign had not come.[51]

The day before that selected date the sign had not yet come.[52] The prophet Nephi prayed fervently.[53]

That very night, at the setting of the sun, it still remained light as though it were day.[54] Those opposing the believers were stunned, the believers were spared,[55] and continued in their faith that the promised Messiah had now been born into the world.

Sacrifice and Atonement

One of the central teachings by prophets in the Book of Mormon is that without the suffering and atonement of Jesus Christ, all mankind would be lost. One such prophet, Benjamin, as mentioned above, prophesied that blood would come from every pore of the Lord's body so great would be the anguish for the wickedness and the abominations of His people.[56]

Accessing the redeeming power of this Atonement had a condition—repentance,[57] or "faith unto repentance",[58] as it is referred to. Those who would believe and have faith in Jesus Christ and His power to spiritually heal them would come unto Him, confessing and abandoning their sins.[59]

All who would partake of Christ's mercy would choose to come unto Him, and to repent of their sins. If they sincerely repented, Jesus Christ would forgive them.[60] and they could start anew in striving to love and follow Him, and be born again[61] through water[62] and the Spirit.[63]

Crucifixion and Death

The Book of Mormon tells of great storms, earthquakes, and destructions at the time of Christ's death.[64] In the process, the wicked were destroyed[65] while the more righteous, yet still imperfect, were preserved.[66]

The account speaks of such great storms and earthquakes that some cities burned with fire,[67] others were buried,[68] and some were sunk into the sea.[69]

Resurrection

The resurrection of Jesus Christ is the highlight of the Book of Mormon. As indicated above, Jesus Christ personally came to the Americas, descending out of the heavens, appearing to the people, and inviting them to come to him and feel the prints of the nails in his hands and his feet, which they did.

The visit of Jesus Christ, following his resurrection, to the Americas is described in great detail upon his first visit to the people.[70] The Book of Mormon also indicates, however, that He made additional visits to his disciples.[71]

Teachings

The Book of Mormon records prophetic teachings of the Old Testament, citing large passages from the writings of the Old Testament prophet Isaiah.[72]

It records in great detail the Messianic prophecies[73] and the teachings of God to His people to trust in Him[74] and repent of their wrong-doings.[75] On occasion, angels appear to these prophets and give them further instruction to teach the people.[76]

These teachings include the importance of faith in God and Jesus Christ,[77] repenting of one's sins,[78] being baptized by immersion,[79] and receiving and following the Holy Ghost.[80]

A key teaching of the prophets is a description of the process by which all mankind can study, pray and learn by the Holy Ghost what the truth about and from God is.[81]

When Jesus Christ visited the people in America, he taught them many principles He had taught in the Sermon on the Mount,[82] including that mankind should show mercy to others,[83] be peacemakers,[84] not judge others,[85] and pray to the Father in His name.[86]

Miracles

The Book of Mormon speaks of many faithful receiving miracles from God.[87] Those miracles include crossing an ocean with the protecting hand of God in the face of treacherous storms,[88] a vision of Jesus Christ and his twelve apostles,[89] a remarkable public prophecy of corruption and the murder of the chief judge,[90] the healing by Jesus Christ of the lame and sick among the people,[91] Christ's prayer and blessing upon all the little children,[92] a heavenly manifestation of angels ministering to such children,[93] remarkable divine escapes from prisons,[94] unlikely victories in military battles,[95] and the raising from the dead by the prophet of his brother.[96]

Priesthood

The Book of Mormon on multiple occasions speaks of the ordaining of priests and teachers[97] to instruct the people regarding repentance and remission of sins.[98]

Jesus Christ when he came to the Americas chose twelve disciples[99] who functioned much as the apostles did in Jerusalem.

It speaks of sacramental prayer[100] offered by the priests in remembrance of the body and blood of Jesus Christ.

It teaches the importance of baptism[101] and that it should be performed by one having authority[102] and by immersion.[103] The form of baptism was specifically prescribed by Jesus Christ when he came.[104]

The Book of Mormon is somewhat unique in specifically teaching that little children should not be baptized[105]—that they do not need to be[106]—and that they have no sin.[107] It states that little children that die without baptism are "alive in Christ"[108] and are all saved.[109]

Establishment of Church

There are multiple passages and chapters in the Book of Mormon indicating that believers were part of a church, or a congregation of believers.

One of the first examples comes when Jacob is teaching the people gathered together at the temple.[110] He admonishes them for their pride,[111] and then strongly condemns the practice among some to have more than one wife.[112]

Speaking of their responsibilities in the church or priesthood, Jacob says,

> *"For I Jacob , and my brother Joseph had been consecrated priests and teachers of this people, by the hand of Nephi.*
>
> *"And we did magnify our office unto the Lord, taking upon us the responsibility, answering the sins of the people upon our own heads if we did not teach them the word of God with all diligence; wherefore, by laboring with our might their blood might not come upon our garments; otherwise their blood would come upon our garments, and we would not be found spotless at the last day."[113]*

Alma, a prophet, said this of his consecration as a high priest over the church:

> *"I, Alma, having been consecrated by my father, Alma, to be a high priest over the church of God, he having power and authority from God to do these things, behold I say unto you that he began to establish a church in the land which was in the borders of Nephi; yea, the land which was called the land of Mormon; yea, and he did baptize his brethren in the waters of Mormon."[114]*

Alma undertook his responsibility to minister and preach to those of the church in Zarahemla,[115] Gideon,[116] and Melek.[117] He also preached the word in Ammonihah.[118]

Alma speaking of others being called as priests, or high priests, said,

> "And those priests were ordained after the order of his Son, in a manner that thereby the people might know in what manner to look forward to his Son for redemption.
>
> "And this is the manner after which they were ordained—being called and prepared from the foundation of the world according to the foreknowledge of God, on account of their exceeding faith and good works…."[119]

When Jesus Christ visited the people, He called Nephi and gave him *"power that ye shall baptize this people when I am again ascended into heaven. And again the Lord called others, and said unto them likewise; and he gave unto them power to baptize…."[120]*

"And it came to pass that when Jesus had spoken these words unto Nephi, and to those who had been called, (now the number of them who had been called, and received power and authority to baptize, was twelve) and behold, he stretched forth his hand unto the multitude, and cried unto them, saying: Blessed are ye if ye shall give heed unto the words of these twelve whom I have chosen from among you to minister unto you, and to be your servants; and unto them I have given power that they may baptize you with water…."[121]

Centuries later it was clear that the practice of baptism into a congregational church was still ongoing.

One prophet, named Moroni taught,

> *"And now I speak concerning baptism. Behold, elders, priests, and teachers were baptized; and they were not baptized save they brought forth fruit meet that they were worthy of it.*

> "Neither did they receive any unto baptism save they came forth with a broken heart and a contrite spirit, and witnessed unto the church that they truly repented of all their sins.
>
> "And none were received unto baptism save they took upon them the name of Christ, having a determination to serve him to the end.
>
> "And after they had been received unto baptism, and were wrought upon and cleansed by the power of the Holy Ghost, they were numbered among the people of the church of Christ; and their names were taken, that they might be remembered and nourished by the good word of God, to keep them in the right way, to keep them continually watchful unto prayer, relying alone upon the merits of Christ, who was the author and the finisher of their faith."[122]

Marriage and Children

As referenced earlier, two specific teachings of the Book of Mormon which are somewhat unique are the following:

1. Men should only have one wife.

Jacob pointedly taught the following:

> "Wherefore, my brethren, hear me, and hearken to the word of the Lord: For there shall not any man among you have save it be one wife; and concubines he shall have none."[123]

The Torah, Nevi'im, and Ketuvim all allow the practice of men having more than one wife.[124] The New Testament, however, speaks against the practice—at least in the case of bishops.[125]

The Book of Mormon goes beyond the New Testament injunction, and roundly rejects the practice of multiple wives. It implies the practice, unless commanded by God, is a "whoredom", an abomination before the Lord.[126] Without speaking specifically to the many practices found in the Torah, Nevi'im, Ketuvim, and the Law of Moses itself,[127] the Book of Mormon does state that only God can command His people to take more than one wife,[128] but that otherwise it is strictly prohibited.[129]

2. Children are innocent, and do not need baptism.

Mormon taught,

"Listen to the words of Christ, your Redeemer, your Lord and your God. Behold, I came into the world not to call the righteous but sinners to repentance; the whole need no physician, but they that are sick; wherefore, little children are whole, for they are not capable of committing sin; wherefore the curse of Adam is taken from them in me...."[130]

"I know that it is solemn mockery before God, that ye should baptize little children...."[131]

"For awful is the wickedness to suppose that God saveth one child because of baptism, and the other must perish because he hath no baptism...."[132]

"For behold that all little children are alive in Christ, and also all they that are without the law. For the power of redemption cometh on all them that have no law; wherefore, he that is not condemned, or he that is under no condemnation, cannot repent; and unto such baptism availeth nothing—"[133]

Temples

The Book of Mormon does not speak specifically of temple worship details. It does, however, mention at least three different temples throughout its history. There may have been others but three are referenced mostly in an inadvertent way.

It is stated that one of the temples was built after the manner of Solomon's Temple.[134]

Another states that the people were gathered together to hear their prophet / king instruct them and give them a name.[135]

And the last mentioned was when the people had gathered to the temple in Zarahemla[136] and the resurrected Jesus Christ descended out of the heavens and appeared to them.[137] He showed them His resurrected body, which they all felt with their hands.[138] He then taught them, instructed them on the proper procedures for baptism,[139] and gave them a sermon very similar to that found in the Sermon on the Mount in Jerusalem.[140]

As a part of his visit to this people He invited them to present all their sick and afflicted and He healed them.[141]

Furthermore, He invited them to put forth their children whom He prayed for in a way incapable of mortal description.[142] He blessed the children.[143] Angels encircled them with fire and they all shed tears of divine joy and love.[144]

Gathering of Israel

The Book of Mormon has several chapters devoted to accounts of missionaries sent forth to preach the word of God to others,[145] including those esteemed as enemies.[146]

One predominant account is of the sons of Mosiah who asked permission of their father to go forth among the Lamanites to teach them the gospel.[147] The father prayed and asked God for guidance.[148] In response, God told their father, Mosiah, to allow them to go and that he would protect them.[149]

Their travels included some great perils including at one point an individual with a raised sword ready to kill Ammon,[150] one of the sons. But prior to his lowering the sword in a blow of death to Ammon he was struck dead.[151] Ammon was thus protected. So also others of the missionaries were imprisoned but miraculously rescued.[152]

The astonishing segment of these missionary accounts is the conversion of thousands,[153] including leaders—kings[154]—who humbly repented of their sins and sought God's forgiveness.[155] In the end, thousands were baptized into the church and remained faithful thereafter.[156]

One of the principles set forth by the Book of Mormon is the value of every soul—every one. These sons of Mosiah, it is said, "could not stand" the thought "that any human soul should perish."[157] Motivated by a selfless love of others, the missionaries thus sacrificed so much, including thirst, hunger, fatigue,[158] and much more that others might come unto Jesus Christ and enjoy a fresh relief of forgiveness for past sins, and thereafter strive to live lives according to God's laws.

Prophecies of Messiah's Second Coming

The Book of Mormon contains multiple prophecies of two comings of the Messiah.[159]

The first coming relates to his birth and life on earth.[160]

The second coming relates to his glorious descension from the heavens at the end of the present world.[161]

Some of these prophecies are found in the teachings of Isaiah and are also found in the Nevi'im, such as:

"[T]he glory of his majesty shall smite them, when he ariseth to shake terribly the earth...";[162]

"[D]ay of the Lord cometh...he shall destroy the sinners thereof out of it...";[163] *and,*

"[T]he glory of his majesty shall smite them, when he ariseth to shake terribly the earth..."[164]

Other prophecies are unique to the American prophets, such as:

"[D]ay when I shall come in my glory in the clouds of heaven...";[165]
"[T]hen shall the wicked be cast out..."[166]

Commandments

Throughout the Book of Mormon various commandments of God are taught, including, but not limited to,

1. The importance of prayer;[167]
2. Encouragement to study the word of God;[168]
3. Being humble, meek, and lowly;[169]
4. Having faith in Jesus Christ;[170]
5. Repenting of one's sins;[171]
6. Being baptized by immersion by one having proper priesthood authority;[172]
7. Following the Holy Ghost;[173]
8. Husbands being morally chaste and faithful to their wife;[174]
9. The importance of men having just one wife;[175]
10. The Ten Commandments;[176]
11. Judging not;[177]
12. Being charitable and giving to the beggar;[178]
13. Serving other people;[179]
14. Having hope;[180] and,
15. Following the prophets.[181]

Sacrifice

The Book of Mormon makes reference to sacrifices and the Law of Moses.[182]

It also makes references to an ending of the Law of Moses by the sacrifice of Jesus Christ.[183]

The Book of Mormon teaches that the sacrifices before Jesus Christ were commanded by God as a type and symbol of the upcoming sacrifice of Jesus Christ.[184] It further teaches that once Jesus Christ had suffered for all mankind,[185] that all might be forgiven on conditions of repentance,[186] that the sacrifice commanded as part of the Law of Moses was thus to end.[187]

CHAPTER 4

New Testament of Jesus Christ

New Testament of Jesus Christ

Foremost among all of the New Testament teachings is that Jesus Christ is the promised Messiah,[1] the literal Son of God,[2] that he descended from above to live a mortal life,[3] taught the gospel and commandments of His Father,[4] and organized His church with twelve apostles.[5] He then, in the supreme act of all of mortality suffered for the sins of all mankind[6] that they might follow His teachings[7] and repent[8] and come unto Him.[9] He was then unjustly accused and tried,[10] and as a lamb brought to the slaughter[11] was slain on a hill called Golgotha.[12]

The New Testament then tells of His miraculous resurrection from the dead wherein he left the tomb of burial,[13] appeared unto Mary[14] and many others[15] and then ascended into heaven as the attending angels promised He would return.[16]

The New Testament itself speaks to several important topics, including the following.

God the Father

Jesus Christ shows complete and absolute loyalty to His Eternal Father, God.[17] He worships Him. He loves Him. He trusts Him. He prays to Him[18] and He thanks Him[19] for hearing and answering Him. He pleads to Him in His time of greatest trial and agony,[20] referring to Him in the Aramaic of "Papa."[21]

His love of His Father is so complete that on multiple occasions, so many of them recorded in the gospel of John, He shuns the approval of the world and remains, instead, loyal to His Father.[22]

While upon the cross He makes a plea to His Father in behalf of His crucifiers that they might be forgiven because "they know not what they do."[23]

When His mortal ministry is complete, His agony and Atonement completed, He humbly says to His Father upon the cross, "Father, into thy hands I commend my Spirit."[24] Then He gave up the ghost—he died.[25]

Jesus Christ not only loved the Father. He was His literal Son, both spiritually[26] and physically.[27] His spirit body, inside His physical body, was the "Firstborn"[28] of the Father. While the New Testament speaks of all mankind as the "offspring of God",[29] among all these children of the Father only Jesus Christ was the Firstborn, the Senior Spirit or Child of all God's children.

Of all these children, only Jesus Christ's physical body was also the offspring of God the Father. He is thus also called the "Only Begotten",[30] meaning "Only Begotten of God the Father." All the rest of God's children have physical parents from among the long line of ancestors leading back to Adam and Eve, the first parents. Jesus Christ, however, was born of the mortal Mary,[31] but His Father was not Joseph, but God the Father.[32] His conception is to the understanding of mortals miraculous, because Mary "[knew] not a man"[33] when she became pregnant.

Given assurances by an angel that the baby conceived in Mary was of God,[34] Joseph went through with his planned marriage to Mary[35] and "knew her not"[36] until the Baby was born. He then became Jesus Christ's caretaker father here on earth.

Jesus Christ

The Torah, Nevi'im, and Ketuvim speak repeatedly of a Messiah who is to come. In doing so, it speaks of two distinct comings: the first, when He would be born of a virgin[37] Mary in Bethlehem; and the second, when He would come in glory in judgment upon a wicked world.[38]

In total, there are some 50 separate Torah, Nevi'im, and Ketuvim passages describing this Messiah's first coming, life, miracles,

Atonement, crucifixion, and His resurrected body. Such passages can be grouped as follows.

- **Messiah's Birth and Youth:**

1) Virgin shall conceive;
2) Ruler come out of Bethlehem;
3) Rachel weeping for her children, they were not;
4) Call my Son out of Egypt;
5) Star out of Jacob;
6) Righteous Branch;
7) Stem of Jesse;
8) Raise up a Prophet;
9) Prince of Peace;

- **Messiah's Teachings and Ministry:**

10) Prepare ye the way of the Lord, crieth in the wilderness;
11) Put my spirit upon my servant;
12) Open His mouth in parables;
13) No deceit in His mouth;
14) Land of Zebulun and Naphtali, seen a great light;
15) Walked in darkness, saw a great light;
16) Hear, understand not, see, perceive not;
17) Bind up the broken hearted;
18) Thy King cometh;
19) King cometh, riding upon an ass;
20) Precious cornerstone;
21) The stone builders refused;

- **Messiah's Miracles:**

22) Waves stilled;
23) Storm calmed;

- **Messiah's Suffering:**

24) Afflicted in all their afflictions;
25) Bruised him;
26) Stricken for the transgressions of His people;
27) Wounded for transgressions;
28) Borne our griefs, carried our sorrows;

- **Messiah's Betrayal to Death:**

29) Friend "lifted up his heel";
30) Sold for silver;
31) Thirty pieces of silver;
32) Hated without a cause;
33) Lamb brought to the slaughter;
34) Smite the Shepherd, sheep are scattered;
35) Gave back to the smiters;
36) Giveth His cheek;
37) Smiteth him;
38) Nail in His holy, sure place;
39) Hands pierced;
40) Numbered with the transgressors;
41) Mocked, "let him deliver him";
42) Mocked, "wag his head";
43) Given vinegar to drink;
44) "My God, my God, why hast thou forsaken" me;
45) Into God's hand commits His spirit;
46) Pierced;
47) Not one bone is broken;
48) His garments will be parted; Lots cast upon His vesture;
49) Grave with the wicked; and,
50) Cut off.

Here are the references for each of these 50 Torah, Nevi'im and Ketuvim prophecies, as well as their New Testament fulfillment:

(#) Prophecy / Fulfillment	Book	Chapter	Verse
(1) a virgin shall conceive	Isaiah	7	14
virgin shall be with child…bring forth a son…call his name Emmanuel…interpreted…God with us	Matthew	1	23
(2) thou, Bethlehem..though thou be little…out of thee shall he come forth…ruler in Israel	Micah	5	2
thou Bethlehem…art not the least among the princes of Juda…come a Governor…rule	Matthew	2	6
(3) in Ramah, lamentation, and bitter weeping; Rachel weeping for her children…they were not	Jeremiah	31	15
Herod…slew all the children that were in Bethlahem	Matthew	2	16
(4) I loved him, and called my son out of Egypt	Hosea	11	1
was there until the death of Herod…fulfilled which was spoken…Out of Egypt…called my son	Matthew	2	15
(5) come a Star out of Jacob	Numbers	24	17
Jesus Christ	Matthew	1	1
Abraham begat Isaac…begat Jacob…Judah…Phares	Matthew	1	2
(6) righteous Branch	Jeremiah	23	5
Jesus Christ	Matthew	1	1
(7) stem of Jesse	Isaiah	11	1
Jesus Christ	Matthew	1	1
Salmon begat Booz of Rachab…Booz begat Obed of Ruth…Obed begat Jesse	Matthew	1	5
And Jesse begat David the king; and David the king begat Solomon	Matthew	1	6

(8) The Lord thy God will raise up unto thee a Prophet from the midst…hearken	Deuteronomy	18	15
Prophet…like unto thee	Deuteronomy	18	18
The woman saith unto him, Sir, I perceive that thou art a prophet	John	4	19
(9) his name shall be called…Prince of Peace	Isaiah	9	6
let not your heart be troubled, neither let it be afraid	John	14	27
(10) voice of him…crieth in the wilderness, Prepare ye the way of the Lord, make straight	Isaiah	40	3
one crying in the wilderness, Prepare ye the way of the Lord, make his paths straight	Luke	3	4
writen in the prophets…I send my messenger…prepare thy way before thee	Mark	1	2
voice of one crying in the wilderness, Prepare ye the way of the Lord…paths straight	Mark	1	3
(11) To open the blind eyes, to bring out the prisoners from the prison	Isaiah	42	7
Behold my servant…beloved…put my spirit upon him…he shall shew judgment…Gentiles	Matthew	12	18
(12) I will open my mouth in a parable	Psalm	78	2
Watch ye therefore: for ye know not when the master of the house cometh	Mark	13	35
(13) neither was any deceit in his mouth	Isaiah	53	9
I am the way…truth…life: no man cometh unto the Father, but by me	John	14	6
(14) land of Zebulun…land of Naphtali…people walked in darkness have seen a great light	Isaiah	9	1
he came and dwelt in Capernaum…in the borders of Zabulon and Nephthalim	Matthew	4	13

might be fulfilled…Esaias…land of Zabulon…Nephthalim…people…saw great light	Matthew	4	14
The land of Zabulon, and the land of Nephtalim, by the way of the sea	Matthew	4	15
(15) walked in darkness…see a…light	Isaiah	9	2
The people which sat in darkness saw great light	Matthew	4	16
(16) Hear ye indeed, but understand not…see ye indeed, but perceive not	Isaiah	6	9
prophecy of Esaias…hearing ye shall hear…not understand…seeing…see...not perceive	Matthew	13	14
(17) he hath sent me to bind up the brokenhearted, to proclaim liberty to the captives	Isaiah	61	1
Neither do I condemn thee: go, and sin no more	John	8	11
(18) behold, thy King cometh unto thee	Zechariah	9	9
hosanna: Blessed is the King of Israel	John	12	13
Behold, thy King cometh unto thee, meek, and sitting upon an ass, and a colt	Matthew	21	5
they that followed, cried, saying, Hosanna; Blessed is he that cometh in the name…Lord	Mark	11	9
Blessed be the kingdom of our father David, that cometh in the name of the Lord: Hosanna	Mark	11	10
(19) riding upon an ass, and upon a colt	Zechariah	9	9
Jesus, when he had found a young ass, sat thereon	John	12	14
ass…colt…hosanna	Matthew	21	7
ye shall find a colt tied, whereon never man sat; loose him, and bring him	Mark	11	2
(20) precious corner stone	Isaiah	28	16

The stone which the builders rejected...same is become the head of the corner	Matthew	21	42
(21) stone...builders refused	Psalm	118	22
The stone which the builders rejected...same is become the head of the corner	Matthew	21	42
This is the stone which was set at nought of you builders...become...head...corner	Acts	4	11
(22) waves...thou stillest them	Psalm	89	9
peace, be still...wind ceased, and there was a great calm	Mark	4	39
(23) he maketh the storm a calm	Psalm	107	29
peace, be still...wind ceased, and there was a great calm	Mark	4	39
(24) Saviour...he bare them, and carried them all the days of old	Isaiah	63	9
his sweat was as it were great drops of blood falling down to the ground	Luke	22	44
(25) pleased the Lord to bruise him	Isaiah	53	10
shewed by...prophets...Christ should suffer, he hath so fulfilled	Acts	3	18
(26) for the transgression of my people was he stricken	Isaiah	53	8
his sweat was as it were great drops of blood falling down to the ground	Luke	22	44
(27) he was wounded for our transgressions	Isaiah	53	5
his sweat was as it were great drops of blood falling down to the ground	Luke	22	44
(28) Surely he hath borne our griefs, and carried our sorrow	Isaiah	53	4
Esaias...Himself took our infirmities, and bare our sicknesses	Matthew	8	17
(29) mine...friend...lifted up his heel	Psalm	41	9
Then one of the twelve, called Judas Iscariot, went unto the chief priests	Matthew	26	14
(30) sold the righteous for silver	Amos	2	6

thirty pieces of silver	Matthew	26	15
(31) So they weighed for my price thirty pieces of silver	Zechariah	11	12
(31) And I took the thirty pieces of silver, and cast them to the potter in the house of the Lord	Zechariah	11	13
fulfilled…Jeremy the prophet…they took the thirty pieces of silver, the price	Matthew	27	9
(32) They that hate me without a cause	Psalm	69	6
fulfilled that is written in their law, They hated me without a cause	John	15	25
(33) I was like a lamb or an ox that is brought to the slaughter	Jeremiah	11	19
Caiaphas	Matthew	26	57
(34) smite the shepherd, and the sheep shall be scattered	Zechariah	13	7
Then all the disciples forsook him	Matthew	26	56
And they all forsook him, and fled	Mark	14	50
be offended because of me this night..I will smite the shepherd…sheep…scattered	Matthew	14	27
be offended because of me this night…written…smite the shepherd…scattered	Matthew	26	31
(35) gave my back to the smiters	Isaiah	50	6
released he Barabbas unto them…scourged Jesus…delivered him to be crucified	Matthew	27	26
Pilate, willing to content the people, released Barabbas…Jesus..scourged him…crucified	Mark	15	15
Pilate therefore took Jesus, and scourged him	John	19	1
(36) he giveth his cheek	Lamentations	3	30
they spit in his face, and buffeted him…others smote him with the palms…hands	Matthew	26	67
(37) smiteth him	Lamentations	3	30

they spit in his face, and buffeted him…others smote him with the palms…hands	Matthew	26	67
(38) nail in his holy place	Ezra	9	8
(38) nail in a sure place	Isaiah	22	23
(38) out of him came forth…the nail	Zechariah	10	4
I shall see in his hands the print of the nails, and put my finger into the print of the nails	John	20	25
(39) they pierced my hands	Psalm	22	16
I shall see in his hands the print of the nails, and put my finger into the print of the nails	John	20	25
(40) he was numbered with the transgressors	Isaiah	53	12
scripture was fulfilled…he was numbered with the transgressors	Mark	15	28
(41) He trusted on the Lord that he would deliver him: let him deliver him	Psalm	22	8
Save thyself, and come down from the cross	Mark	15	30
Likewise also the chief priests mocking said…with the scribes…saved others; himself	Mark	15	31
(42) wag his head	Jeremiah	18	16
they that passed by railed on him, wagging their heads	Mark	15	29
Save thyself, and come down from the cross	Mark	15	30
(43) They gave me also gall for my meat; and in my thirst they gave me vinegar to drink	Psalm	69	21
one ran and filled a spunge full of vinegar, and put it on a reed, and gave him to drink	Mark	15	34
(44) my God, my God, why hast thou forsaken	Psalm	22	1
Jesus cried with a loud voice…"My God, my God, why hast thou forsaken me?"	Mark	15	36

(45) into thine hand I commit my spirit	Psalm	31	5
Father, into thy hands I commend my spirit	Luke	23	46
(46) they shall look upon me whom they have pierced	Zechariah	12	10
They shall look on him whom they pierced	John	19	37
(47) He keepeth all his bones: not one of them is broken	Psalm	69	21
scripture should be fulfilled, A bone of him shall not be broken	John	19	36
(48) They part my garments among them, and cast lots upon my vesture	Psalm	22	18
they parted his raiment, and cast lots	Luke	23	34
fulfilled...parted my garments among them...upon my vesture did they cast lots	Matthew	27	35
they had crucified him, they parted his garments, casting lots upon them	Mark	15	24
scripture might be fulfilled...They parted my raiment among them...my vesture...cast lots	John	19	24
(49) he made his grave with the wicked...neither was any deceit in his mouth	Isaiah	53	9
with him they crucify two thieves; the one on his right hand, and the other on his left	Mark	15	27
(50) Messiah be cut off	Daniel	9	26
Father, into thy hands I commend my spirit	Luke	23	46

Thus, the New Testament not only records Jesus Christ's divine birth of the virgin Mary in Bethlehem, as prophesied centuries earlier, but it also records the precise fulfilment of every one of the 50 prophecies.

That remarkable fulfillment comes in the Person, Jesus Christ of Nazareth.

The New Testament is thus a sequel to the prophetic writings which preceded it. It is the natural companion to the Torah, Nevi'im, and Ketuvim, recording the actual birth, life, teachings, miracles, suffering and Atonement, death, and resurrection of the promised Messiah.

It is a witness, or Testament—a New Testament—that the Messiah had in fact been sent by God to earth. It is a witness that Jesus Christ is the Messiah, the actual divine Son of God the Father.

It is a witness that the Torah, Nevi'im, and Ketuvim are true prophecies sent by God.

Commandments and Teachings

The four gospels of the New Testament tell so many of the teachings of Jesus Christ. When His ministry began, he started by calling people to repent.[39]

He taught people to have faith in Him,[40] to repent,[41] and to be baptized[42]—setting the example Himself as He was baptized by John the Baptist.[43]

His most famous teachings came at the Sermon on the Mount where he taught listeners that

Blessed are,
- a) The poor in spirit: for theirs is the kingdom of heaven;[44]
- b) They that mourn: for they shall be comforted;[45]
- c) The meek: for they shall inherit the earth;[46]
- d) They which do hunger and thirst after righteousness: for they shall be filled;[47]
- e) The merciful: for they shall obtain mercy;[48]
- f) The pure in heart: for they shall see God;[49]
- g) The peacemakers: for they shall be called the children of God;[50]
- h) They which are persecuted for righteousness' sake: for theirs is the kingdom of heaven;[51]

i) When men shall revile you, and persecute you, and shall say all manner of evil against you falsely, for my sake.[52]

He also taught His listeners were the "light of the world"[53] and that they should not hide that light, but put it on a candlestick so that others "may see your good works and glorify your Father which is in heaven."[54]

He taught a higher gospel law than the law of Moses and compared and connected the two. He stated that,

1) The Law of Moses taught "Thou shalt not kill";[55] but He taught we should not be "angry with [our] brother without a cause";[56]
2) The Law of Moses taught "Thou shalt not commit adultery";[57] but He taught we should not "look on a woman to lust after her";[58]
3) The Law of Moses taught that whosoever shall put away his wife should give her a writing of divorcement;[59] but he taught that a wife should not be put away save for the cause of fornication;[60]
4) The Law of Moses taught that one should not "forswear thyself, but shalt perform unto the Lord thine oaths";[61] but He taught that we should "[s]wear not at all; neither by heaven; for it is God's throne: Nor by the earth; for it is his footstool: neither by Jerusalem; for it is the city of the great King."[62] He taught that our communication and commitments should be simple and trustworthy, "Yea" or "Nay."[63]
5) The Law of Moses taught that wrongdoing should be punished an "eye for an eye and a tooth for a tooth";[64] but He taught that we "resist not evil",[65] and even go further and "if any man will sue thee at the law, and take away thy coat, let him have thy cloak also."[66]

He also taught that we should love our enemies,[67] and that we should be perfect, "even as your Father which is in Heaven is perfect."[68]

He also taught men how to pray, commending them to call upon God the Father, acknowledging his power and might, asking for our daily bread, protection from temptation, and that God would forgive us as we forgive others. Many know this teaching as the Lord's Prayer.[69]

He taught men to "judge not, that ye be not judged",[70] and said that "with what judgment ye judge, ye shall be judged."[71]

He also taught that we should,

- a) Do our alms in secret;
- b) Pray in secret to our Father who seeeth in secret;
- c) Use not vain repetitions when we pray;
- d) When we fast appear not unto men to fast;
- e) Lay not up for ourselves treasures upon earth, but treasures in heaven; and,
- f) Keep our eye single, that our whole body shall be full of light. He also taught that,
- g) No man can serve two masters;
- h) Seek first the kingdom of God, and His righteousness; and,
- i) All things whatsoever ye would that men should do to you, do ye even so unto them..

It is understood by some New Testament followers that the Mosaic Law and the Higher Law were both given by Jesus Christ, with the former being a schoolmaster in preparation for the latter.

Sacrifice and Atonement

The New Testament tells of the Atonement of Jesus Christ, where Christ, as the prophesied lamb offered without blemish, in submissive prayer to God the Father, took upon Him the punishment, pain, grief and sorrows of all mankind. So heavy was the pain of such vicarious suffering for the sins of all men and women, that Jesus Christ in agony bled from every pore of his body.

Jesus Christ in prayer to the Father had asked that "if possible", that the cup of pain and suffering be removed from Him. Yet, in perhaps the greatest act of recorded humility, He also surrendered to the Father that "nevertheless, Thy will be done."

The sacrifice of Jesus Christ enabled all mankind if they met the conditions set by the Savior to be forgiven of their sins. Without His suffering, mankind was left with the consequences of their own sinful choices. With the stain of guilt, divine redemption was not possible and man was trapped by his own sin and forever barred from the presence of God.

Not only did mankind have a vital interest in the power of Jesus Christ's sacrifice, but so did God the Father Himself. All mankind were the spirit offspring—the children—of God the Father. In order for them to have the growth and happiness that comes from practicing free will with knowledge between right and wrong, there would also need to be provided a way that their sinful mistakes could be atoned for and eliminated. Otherwise, their mortal experience with the exercise of free will would come at a cost of eternal stain. All mankind would then be left outside of God's presence, unworthy and unable to reenter His presence.

With the Atonement, mankind could exercise their free will to satisfy the redemptive conditions of Christ's grace by repenting and being baptized and thereafter striving to love God and keep His commandments. They would not merit His grace, but they would receive it as an act of divine mercy to those of God's children who humbly sought to change their ways and follow Christ.

Miracles

The New Testament records multiple miracles performed by Jesus Christ, including,

1) Changing water into wine at a wedding feast where the wine had run out;

2) Blessing a very small amount of bread and fishes so that they somehow increased in quantity to feed thousands;
3) Casting out evil spirits;
4) Healing the blind so they could see;
5) Healing the lame;
6) Healing the deaf so they could hear;
7) Raising those who had died so they were alive again; and,
8) Replacing and healing the bloodied ear of a soldier cut off by the sword so it was whole again.

Considered by many as His preeminent miracle was His choice and ability to suffer and bleed from every pore to pay an unfathomable price for the sins of others, that they might repent and be forgiven.

The New Testament indicates that after Christ was crucified and died, that His body was placed in a tomb. It records the miraculous event on the third day of His resurrection where Christ came to life, appeared to many, charged His disciples to love others and to proclaim His gospel throughout the world. He then ascended into the heavens.

Priesthood

The New Testament records that Jesus Christ ordained twelve men as His apostles. When one of these apostles died, the remaining apostles prayed to know whom God had called to replace him and serve as an apostle with the others.

It also speaks of prophets, seventy, deacons, teachers, and priests. It speaks of calling the elders to anoint with oil and bless an individual when sick.

The New Testament teaches that in the latter-days two prophets will be in Jerusalem, and will be slain by the people, and then resurrected to life again.

The New Testament also speaks that Jesus Christ is the great high priest who through His sacrifice enabled the remission of our sins and our coming unto God.

Establishment of Church

Not only did Jesus Christ give priesthood authority to others, but He specifically charged them to go unto all the world to teach and baptize others.

He commanded His followers to meet regularly and partake of bread and wine in remembrance of His body and blood, that they might remember Him.

The New Testament states that Jesus Christ gave the priesthood officers to help saints—his followers—be perfected, and for the "work of the ministry" and for the "edifying of the body of Christ." It states that such were to be given "till we all come in the unity of the faith."

Temples

The New Testament tells of Christ's calling the temple in Jerusalem as His "Father's house." It also tells of the apostles going to the temple after the resurrection of Jesus Christ.

In the Book of Revelation it speaks of temples in the last days.

In the Gospels of the New Testament it tells of Jesus Christ's cleansing of the temple from those who made it a place of business rather than a place of worship.

In Hebrews it speaks of the holy of holies and how it is that Jesus Christ enables us to enter into the presence of God.

Crucifixion and Death

The New Testament tells how Christ was betrayed by Judas, one of His twelve apostles, arrested, beaten, mocked, and then condemned to death by Pilate. Another was compelled to carry His cross to the place of his crucifixion. There He was nailed to the cross and left hanging to die together with two thieves, one on his right side and the other on his left.

In a stunning account, while He was suffering on the cross, the New Testament tells how Jesus Christ was nevertheless concerned for his mother and gave charge to John to care for her.

He also plead to God in His agony that He would forgive those who crucified Him, stating that "they know not what they do."

Resurrection

The New Testament records that Jesus Christ suffered for the sins of mankind in Gethsemane, was betrayed, arrested, mocked, tried, and sentenced to be crucified.

He was crucified and voluntarily "gave up the ghost".

While dead the book of 1 Peter teaches that Jesus Christ went to the spirits in the spirit world and initiated the teaching of the gospel to them that were dead.

On the third day of His death, early in the morning, it records that Mary and other women went to the tomb where he was laid. But upon arriving, they encountered two angels at the opening to the tomb with the great stone rolled away. The angels announced to the visitors that Jesus Christ was not there, "for He is risen, as he said. Come, see the place where the Lord lay. And go quickly, and tell his disciples that he is risen from the dead."

They did so. Peter and John ran to the tomb but found not Jesus Christ. But they did go into the sepulcher and saw the linen clothes lying and the "napkin, that was about his head, not lying with the linen clothes, but wrapped together in a place by itself."

Then the disciples went away.

Mary, however, stood without at the sepulcher weeping, after the disciples had left.

She looked into the sepulcher and saw "two angels, in white sitting, the one at the head, and the other at the feet, where the body of Jesus had lain."

They said unto her "Woman, why weepest thou? She said unto them, Because they have taken away my Lord, and I know not where they have laid him."

And when she had thus said, she turned herself back, and saw Jesus standing, and knew not that it was Jesus.

Jesus saith unto her, "Woman, why weepest thou? Whom sleekest thou? She, supposing him to be the gardener, saith unto him, "Sir, if thou have borne him hence, tell me where thou hast laid him, and I will take him away."

Jesus saith unto her, "Touch me not; for I am not yet ascended to my Father: but go to my brethren, and say unto them, I ascend unto my Father, and your Father; and to my God, and your God."

And as they went to tell his disciples, behold, Jesus met them, saying, "All hail. And they came and held him by the feet, and worshipped him."

Mary Magdalene came and told the disciples that she had seen the Lord, and that he had spoken these things unto her.

Gathering of Israel

The New Testament describes a parable taught by Jesus of the marriage of the king's son. In this parable, Jesus Christ teaches that the "kingdom of heaven is like unto a certain king, which made marriage for his son." The king "sent forth his servants to call them that were bidden to the wedding: and they would not come."

The invited guests "made light of it, and went their ways, one to his farm, another to his merchandise." Subsequently, the king said:

> *"Go ye therefore into the highways, and as many as ye shall find, bid to the marriage. So those servants went out into the highways, and gathered together all as many as they found, both bad and good: and the weding was furnished with guests."*

Similarly, the New Testament teaches that many of Israel by birth have rejected the Messiah, that a great gathering among both "Jew and Gentile" shall occur. The Jews who reject Jesus Christ will no longer be of Israel. The Gentiles who accept Jesus Christ will be "adopted" in to the House of Israel.

By so teaching, the New Testament explains that "Israel" is more defined by those who make Abrahamic covenants, than by those who are Abraham's descendants.

Warnings of Apostasy

The New Testament gives warning of a time of apostasy. The first verses, in 2 Thessalonians 2:1-3 indicates that the "coming of our Lord Jesus Christ…shall not come, except there come a falling away first."

The second passage is found in 1 Timothy 4:1-3 and states that "in the latter times some shall depart from the faith, giving head to seducing spirits."

Some, however, believe that Christ's words to Peter would prevent the Church from ever going astray. Others, however, believe that the protection of the Church was not dependent on the person Peter, but instead on the principle of ongoing divine guidance to the Church.

Redeemer

Through the Atonement of Jesus Christ, all mankind may be redeemed from their lost and fallen state. Because all mankind would sin, and make mistakes as they sought to follow God, a means of repentance and forgiveness was vital.

The New Testament teaches that Jesus Christ is this Redeemer. Through Him, regardless of what sins one may have committed, one could turn his life around—again and again as needed—and seek each time to love and follow Jesus Christ more fully.

The Redeemer brought mercy to all who would come unto Christ and accept of His kind pathway forward.

Because the grace of Jesus Christ would be available not just once, but multiple times in one's life, men and women could continue their mortal experiment with free will, learning as they go and choosing a higher and happier way of living, by seeking to follow Jesus Christ with all their heart.

Prophecies of Redeemer's 1st Coming and 2nd Coming

The New Testament records some 50 instances when Jesus Christ fulfills Torah, Nevi'im, and Ketuvim prophecies of the Messiah.

It thus stands as a clear witness that Jesus Christ in deed is the promised Messiah, and that He is the Son of God.

CHAPTER 5

The Holy Qur'an

The Holy Qur'an

The Quran was written over about a 23-year period from 610 a.d. to 632 a.d. Muslims believe the Quran is revelation Muhammad received from God incrementally over time as God's prophet.[1]

The Quran actually consists of 114 individual books or chapters, each with a separate name, which are then all compiled together.

The Quran describes God as merciful[2] and just,[3] all-powerful[4] and all-knowing.[5]

It tells of an existence before this life and a meeting where Satan was cast out by God.[6]

It encourages all to believe in God,[7] His Prophet Muhammad,[8] and to obey Them.[9] It recounts numerous signs that God has given and thus encourages people to believe.[10]

The Quran admonishes believers to pray,[11] to give alms to the poor,[12] and to make a journey to Mecca during their lifetime.[13]

The Quran often highlights sharp distinctions between believers and non-believers and teaches believers how they should avoid apostasy and how to interact with non-believers.[14]

It speaks of the faith of ancient Israel,[15] the Torah,[16] and ancient Israel's fall from God's grace.[17]

It relates many details regarding the events of Joseph, son of Israel, and his brothers.[18]

The Quran speaks of multiple prophets, including Moses, Noah, Abraham and Jesus Christ.[19] It indicates that Muhammad also was a prophet,[20] and that he was the "seal of the prophets."[21]

It speaks of Jesus Christ as a favored prophet of God,[22] but indicates that He was not crucified[23] and that "that no soul shall bear the burden of another."[24] It speaks favorably of His gospel and teachings.[25]

It has detailed rules for inheritances,[26] marriages,[27] and women.[28]

It states that all will be resurrected,[29] judged,[30] with the righteous placed in an eternal paradise[31] and the wicked cast into a fiery hell.[32]

God as Merciful and Just, All-Powerful and All-Knowing

The Quran teaches with repeated emphasis that God is merciful, that He is all-powerful, and all-knowing. There are not just a few passages so indicating, but scores of them. Here are just a few:

- **Merciful**

  "The mercy of your Lord is all-encompassing..."[33]
  "[Y]our Lord is the Mighty One the Merciful..."[34]
  "He is the Compassionate, the Merciful..."[35]
  "God is most forgiving and merciful..."[36]
  "Your Lord is swift in retribution; yet surely He is most forgiving and merciful..."[37]

- **All-Powerful**

  "God is strong and all-powerful..."[38]
  "God has power over all things..."[39]
  "I am God, the Powerful, the Wise..."[40]
  "God who is the real Protector, He resurrects the dead, and He has power over all things..."[41]
  "God has the power to will anything..."[42]

- **All-Knowing**

  "God has full knowledge of all things..."[43]
  "God is all pervading and all knowing..."[44]
  "He hears all and knows all..."[45]

"God is infinite and all knowing..."[46]

"He knows everything you do..."[47]

- **Just**

In addition, the Quran states that God is just, always treating His servants right:

"We are never unjust..."[48]

"God never does the least wrong to His servants..."[49]

Existence before this Life, God and Satan

The Quran has a most interesting account of a meeting with God, Adam, angels, and Satan—apparently before this world began.

The only other religious text to refer in some detail to this same meeting is Modern Prophets. The two accounts differ in several ways.

The Quran states that:

1) There was an assembly of angels.[50]

"I had no knowledge of the Exalted Assembly when they argued...."[51]

2) At this assembly, both Adam and Satan were present. God commanded all the angels to bow before Adam, which they did, but Satan refused.[52]

"When We said to the angels, 'Bow down before Adam'...all bowed...except...[Satan]."[53]

"Thereupon the angels prostrated themselves, all of them together, but not Satan."[54]

3) In consequence of his refusal to bow before Adam, Satan was cast out of this Assembly.[55]

"God said, 'Then get out of here; for you are accursed....'"[56]

God, His Prophet Muhammad, and Obedience

- **The Quran speaks of multiple prophets, including:**

Aaron,[57]
Abraham,[58]
David,[59]
Elijah,[60]
Elisha,[61]
Idris,[62]
Isaac,[63]
Ishmael,[64]
Jacob,[65]
Jesus Christ,[66]
John,[67]
Jonah,[68]
Lot,[69]
Moses,[70]
Muhammad,[71] and,
Zachariah.[72]

It says that Muhammad is the "seal of the prophets."[73]

In multiple passages the Quran admonishes that people believe and have faith in God and Muhammad, that they follow and obey Them:

> *"Have faith in God and His Messenger...."[74]*
> *"Obey God and obey the Messenger...."[75]*
> *"[I]f you love God, follow me and God will love you..."[76]*

The Quran states that Muhammad is God's Messenger, and that others before also were His messengers and that He gave revelations to them. It states that before God has brought destruction upon a town, He has always sent a messenger first to warn it.

> "*Muhammad is the Messenger of God….*"[77]
> "*God, the Powerful, the Wise, sends revelation to you….*"[78]
> "*[M]essengers We sent before you [Muhammad]…to whom We made revelations….*"[79]
> "*Never have We destroyed a town without sending down messengers to warn it….*"[80]

Signs

The Quran speaks of many signs which God has given and cites them to encourage belief in God, Muhammad, and the Quran. Among these signs are:

1. Abraham was saved from the fire;
2. Beneficial things grow in the earth;
3. God created the heavens and the earth;
4. God created mankind with a diversity of languages and colours;
5. God created spouses with affection and kindness;
6. God destroyed Sodom and Gomorrah, the people of 'Ad, Salih, and drowned the armies of Egypt
7. The flood upon the people of Noah;
8. The winds which enable the ships to sail;
9. Lightning;
10. Lot and his household were saved;
11. God made night for rest and day for light;
12. Moses divided the Red Sea;
13. Rain causes the earth to stir and swell and gives life to the earth; and,
14. The resurrection.

Prayer, Alms to the Poor, and a Journey

- **Prayer**

The Quran instructs all believers to pray. It encourages the faithful to do so morning and evening.

"[G]lorify your Lord with His praise, before the rising and before the setting of the sun…."

Other times are also proscribed for prayer:

"Say your prayers from the decline of the sun, until nightfall…."

"Say your prayers morning and evening, and during parts of the night…."

Devout followers of the Quran will pray five times daily.

In addition, the Quran states "be constant in prayer."

Prayer is to praise God, ask forgiveness, and to seek guidance. The Quran states that God answers prayers.

It teaches that prayers should be offered sincerely, regularly, kneeling or prostrated, in humility and in secret. Prayer should be prepared for with certain washings and purity. Prayer should be with the face towards the Sacred Mosque.

- **Alms**

The Quran teaches the importance of both prayers and giving alms (or zakats) to the poor:

"[S]ay your prayers and pay the prescribed alms."

"Attend to your prayers and pay the zakat and obey the Messenger, so that you may be shown mercy."

"[K]eep up prayer and to give alms secretly and openly out of what We have given them."

"[D]o not chide the one who asks for help."

"[S]pend in charity."

- **Journey**

The Quran also speaks of a pilgrimage that each believer should perform:

> *"Perform the Hajj and the minor pilgrimage [umrah]...."*
> *"Pilgrimage to the House is a duty to God for anyone who is able to undertake it...."*
> *"Call mankind to the Pilgrimage...."*
> *During the pilgrimage one is encouraged to "fast three days" and "for seven days after his return."*

Believers and Non-Believers

The Quran states that all should believe. They should believe in God, believe in Muhammad as God's prophet, and believe in the Quran as God's revelation through Muhammad.

Many blessings are promised to those who believe, including mercy, a "great reward", forgiveness, and grace.

Also promised believers is an eternal habitation in Paradise, which includes Gardens through which rivers flow, bracelets, reclining couches, fruits, drinks, and virgins.

The Quran states that, "[T]hose who have believed and do good works, they shall be given their reward…full…"

The end of believers will be blissful.

In contrast, a "painful" and "grievous" punishment awaits those who do not believe.

- **How to Believe**

How one believes is also spoken of in the Quran. It first states that,

> *"No soul can believe except by the will of God..."*

> "Had your Lord pleased, all the people on earth would have believed in Him…"
>
> "God heaps ignominy upon those who refuse to believe…"

In addition, the Quran states the importance in believing, of reason, reflection, repentance, worship, praise, not being arrogant, serving His cause, bowing down, and observing limits set by God

Ancient Israel and the Torah

The Quran states that God made a covenant with Israel.

> "God made a covenant with the Children of Israel."

It tells of Israel's time in the wilderness and also in Egypt. It speaks of Moses' speaking with Pharaoh and Pharaoh's refusal to let Israel go. It tells of the plagues brought upon Egypt as a result.

It recounts the parting of the Red Sea to allow Israel to cross as Egyptian armies were pursuing them, and how God then closed the waters to destroy the Egyptians.

It states that God "favoured them over all other people", and that,

> "[i]f they had observed the Torah and the Gospel and that which was revealed unto them from their Lord, they would surely have been nourished from above."

But in the end, the Quran tells of ancient Israel that,

> "they disobeyed and were given to transgression",

And that,

> "[e]vil indeed were their deeds", and "they rejected the signs of God…put the prophets to death."

Joseph and his Brothers

The Quran speaking of Joseph, son of Israel, states that God gave him "right judgement and knowledge." It tells that,

that his brothers conspired to slay him, but Judah said to sell him. It states that,

a) Joseph dreamed his family prostrated themselves before him;
b) Joseph's brothers conspired to slay him;
c) Judah said to sell him;
d) Jospeh was cast into a well;
e) he was found by a caravan;
f) he was sold for a few pieces of silver;
g) Potiphar's wife attempted to seduce him;
h) he would have succumbed, except for a sign given him by God;
i) Potiphar's wife admitted that she tried to seduce him;
j) He was imprisoned;
k) he interpreted the dream of the baker and the butler;
l) he interpreted the dream of Pharaoh;
m) he was reunited with his brothers; and,
n) then, his shirt was taken by his brothers and "cast upon his father's face" and Israel recovered his sight.

Prophets and Revelation

The Quran speaks of multiple prophets and God giving scriptures to them. Among those named are,

Abraham,

Elijah,

Elisha,

Idras,

Isaac,

Ishmael,

Jesus Christ,
John,
Jonah,
Lot,
Muhammad,
Moses, and,
Zachariah.

Referring to Jesus Christ, the Quran says,

> "We gave Jesus, son of Mary, clear signs and strengthened him with the Holy Spirit."
>
> "We gave him the Gospel, which contained guidance and light."

Referring to Muhammad, the Quran says that he is the "seal of the prophets."

The Quran states that not all messengers are spoken of in the Quran, that,

> "We have told you about some messengers sent previously, while We have not yet told you about others."

The Quran states that God does not "punish until We have sent forth a messenger to forewarn them."

Finally, answers to prayers are not limited to prophets, but are available to those who ask God:

> "Call on Me and I will answer your prayers."
>
> "I respond to the call of one who calls."
>
> "Seek help with patience and prayer."

The Quran encourages that we pray with humility, sincerity, and steadfastness:

> "Call on your Lord with humility and in secret."

> "[C]all upon Him, making yourselves sincere."
> "[Be]…steadfast in their prayers."

The Quran reminds us that truth comes from God.

> "It is God who guides to the truth."
> "No one can tell you [the Truth] like the One who is all knowing."
> "[T]ruth belongs to God alone."

Jesus Christ and His Gospel

As already mentioned, in various passages the Quran speaks of Jesus Christ as a prophet:

> "[T]he prophets, from you and Noah, Abraham, Moses, and Jesus, the son of Mary…."

Of Jesus Christ, it speaks of,

A. Revelations given to Him,

> "We believe in what has been given to Moses, Jesus and the prophets from their Lord….";

B. miracles he would perform—healing the blind and raising the dead,

> "[B]y God's leave I will heal the blind and the leper and bring the dead to life…."

C. that He received the gospel from God,

> "We gave him the Gospel, which contained guidance and light…."

D. was strengthened by the Holy Spirit,

> "Jesus…I strengthened you with the holy spirit…."

E. was born of Mary, a virgin,

> *"Jesus, son of Mary…."*
> *"How can I have a son when no man has touched me…neither…unchaste…."*

It is not clear what is meant by one passage referring to Jesus Christ as the Messiah,

> *"His name is the Messiah, Jesus, son of Mary…"*

What is clear are the Quran's teachings that Jesus was not crucified, could not suffer for our sins, and is not the Son of God,

> *"They did not kill him, nor did they crucify him…."*
> *"No bearer of a burden can bear the burden of another…."*
> *"Christians say, "The Messiah is the son of God." These are…baseless utterances…."*

- **Gospel**

As to the gospel, the Quran states,

1) It was given by God,

> *"We gave him the Gospel, which contained guidance and light…."*
> *"I taught you the Book, and wisdom, the Torah and the Gospel…."*

2) The gospel should have been observed,

> *"If they had observed the Torah and the Gospel and what was revealed to them…surely have been nourished."*

> *"People of the Book, you have no ground to stand on until you observe the Torah and the Gospel and what is revealed to you."*

Inheritances, Marriages, and Women

Regarding inheritances, the Quran teaches that,

1) debts shall be paid first;
2) men shall receive double what a woman receives;
3) if orphans or poor are present, they shall be provided for; and,
4) various rules apply to brothers, sisters, parents, and when an individual is childless.

- **Regarding marriages, the Quran teaches that,**

    1) God "did not prescribe monasticism";
    2) believers should not marry an adulterer nor a polytheist;
    3) "good women are for good men", "good men are for good women", and "corrupt men are for corrupt women";
    4) marriage can occur in Paradise;
    5) when the horn of resurrection blows "there will be no ties of relationship between them…neither will they ask about one another", but other passages indicate marriages can continue in Paradise;
    6) as to multiple wives, "[y]ou will never be able to treat your wives with equal fairness", "but do not ignore one wife altogether";
    7) as to an unfaithful wife, "for those from whom you apprehend infidelity…hit them [lightly]";
    8) divorce has multiple rules relating to various waiting periods, maintenance, pregnancy, and nursing; and,
    9) a man is ineligible to marry certain next of kin, including his mother, daughters, sisters, aunts, etc.

- **Regarding women, the Quran teaches that,**

    1) "men are protectors of women";
    2) "men have a rank above them"; and "male is not like a female";
    3) virtuous women are obedient;

4) the "Lord has forbidden indecency";
5) specific rules apply to those who are Muhammad's wives; and,
6) the inheritance of women is to be half as much as men.

Resurrection, Judgment, Paradise and Hell

- ## Resurrection and Judgment

The Quran states that all will be resurrected and return to God,

> *"[Y]ou shall all be resurrected...."*
> *"[A]s for the dead, God will raise them up, and then they will all return to Him...."*

The Quran also indicates that the Day of resurrection is a day of judgment, when angels shall descend, and every human being shall be judged for the good or evil he has done:

> *"Day when the sky will split open with its clouds and the angels are sent down rank upon rank...."*
> *"On the Day of Resurrection, God will judge between you regarding your differences...."*
> *"Day when every human being will find himself faced with all the good...evil...has done...."*

> *"[on that Day] you shall be divided into three groups.... Those on the Right--how blessed are those on the Right!...Those on the Left--how unlucky are those on the Left!..."*

The earth itself will undergo great change,

> *"[T]he mountains are totally shattered and crumble to pieces and become like scattered dust particles....*

- **Paradise and Heaven**

The Quran extensively refers to paradise. These references, however, are not to a place where spirits go awaiting the resurrection.[82]

The Quran's use of the word paradise is to describe an ultimate place of final, favorable judgment and residence.[83]

Paradise is described primarily as a place of very favorable surroundings.

Paradise includes all of the following:

a) light emanating from the inhabitants;[84]
b) no vain or sinful talk, but only words of peace and tranquility;[85]
c) reclining green couches, placed in a row, facing one another;[86]
d) gold and silver bracelets and pearls and clothing of silk;[87]
e) gold and silver vessels and crystal goblets;[88]
f) best residence and finest lodging;[89]
g) finest carpets;[90]
h) abundant fruit;[91]
i) fruit trees;[92]
j) abundant drinks;[93]
k) meat;[94]
l) eternal shade;[95]
m) virgins, primarily with large beautiful, dark eyes, who men can marry;[96]
n) pure women of an equal age;[97]
o) spouses;[98]
p) springs;[99]
q) gardens through which rivers flow;[100]
r) rivers of milk, honey, pure water, and wine;[101] and,
s) a wall of separation, and a gate of entrance.[102]

It is not clear whether the virgins are women from mortality who never married and kept their virginity, or whether they are newly created for the benefit of man. Although one passage seems to indicate that they are newly created.[103]

The Quran also speaks of living with spouses.[104] So seemingly the Quran indicates that marriage for the faithful can be continued into paradise.

It also is not clear whether the women of equal age include or refers to the virgins or the spouses. Nor is it clear what the age of the man is in paradise—the age at the time of his death or something else.

It speaks of inhabitants being honored and a place of bliss, peace, and security.

It does not specifically speak of any joy from personal ongoing change or progress. The happiness from paradise seems primarily externally based and due to a satisfaction of the senses.

Being placed in paradise lasts for eternity.[105]

Those who are permitted to enter paradise include those who:

- a) believe and do good deeds;[106]
- b) believe the revelations and surrender to God;[107]
- c) seek neither self-aggrandizement on the earth nor corruption;[108]
- d) obey God and His Messenger;[109]
- e) are God-fearing;[110]
- f) are righteous;[111] and/or,
- g) are faithful to their trust and promises and attend to prayers.[112]

- **Hell**

The Quran extensively speaks of hell. It describes it as a place of immeasurable and never-ending suffering. Specifically, it describes suffering due to,

- a) fire that scorches the skin of its inhabitants;[114]
- b) persons whose bodies are consumed receiving new bodies so they can continue to suffer;[115]

c) boiling water being poured over the head;[116]
d) boiling and stinking water given to drink so that it tears the bowels;[117]
e) being stuck in a state—neither alive nor dead--so individuals continue to suffer;[118]
f) climbing ascending stairways for fifty thousand years;[119]
g) being fettered by chains and iron collars;[120]
h) being given filthy food that chokes;[121]
i) being given fruit of the Zaqqum tree which boils in the belly;[122] and,
j) scorching wind.[123]

Those to be cast into hell include any of the following individuals who:
a) amassed wealth and hoarded it;[124]
b) denied the Day of Judgement;[125]
c) turned their back on the true faith;[126]
d) denied the truth;[127]
e) followed Satan;[128]
f) wittingly swore to falsehood;[129]
g) consumed orphans' possessions;[130]
h) denied, scorned, derided, or rejected His revelations;[131]
i) denied the Book of Moses;[132]
j) denied the truth;[133]
k) desired the life of this world and its finery;[134]
l) did not believe in Almighty God;[135]
m) disobeyed or opposed God and His Messenger;[136]
n) persecuted the believing and did not repent;[137]
o) did evil deeds;[138]
p) came to the Lord a sinner;[139]
q) killed a believer deliberately;[140]
r) rejected God's signs;[141]

or who were:

- s) transgressors;[142]
- t) arrogant;[143]
- u) evil doers;[144]
- v) hypocrites;[145]
- w) polytheists;[146]
- x) ungrateful and rebellious;[147] or,
- y) Abu Lahab.[148]

Those sent to hell will reside there forever.[149]

Protected from hell, however, will be those who

1) pray and feed the poor;[150]
2) are not the most wicked;[151]
3) fear God;[152] or,
4) He wills.[153]

CHAPTER 6

Modern Prophets

Modern Prophets

Modern Prophets consist of the writings of multiple apostles and prophets of The Church of Jesus Christ of Latter-day Saints.

Included in Modern Prophets are the *Doctrine & Covenants*, *Pearl of Great Price*, *Articles of Faith*, and semi-annual writings of the prophets and apostles as written in the *Ensign* or *Liahona* from October 2011 forward.

Modern Prophets continues the pattern established with Moses in the Torah, and later with Isaiah, Jeremiah, Amos, and Malachi who as prophets received revelations from God and recorded them. That same pattern was also continued in the New Testament and Book of Mormon where apostles and prophets received the word of God and made a record of those revelations.

While the Torah, Book of Mormon, and New Testament all record revelations of prophets regarding the Messiah, the Quran is distinct in not prophesying of a Messiah, nor of Jesus Christ's return. Nevertheless, the Quran does continue the same tradition of recording revelations from God to Muhammad, considered by Quran followers as God's "seal of the prophets."[1]

Modern Prophets presents to the world that prophets are again upon the earth, and like the earlier practices of the Torah, Book of Mormon, and New Testament, God is again speaking to prophets in modern times for the express purpose of restoring His Church[2] and helping the world prepare for His glorious Second Coming.[3]

Modern Prophets itself, which is an un-ended venue of continuing revelations, speaks to several important topics, including the following.

Jesus Christ

Modern Prophets states that Jesus Christ is indeed the Son of God.[4] It joins the New Testament in witnessing that Jesus Christ is the long-awaited Messiah of the Torah.

It speaks of a specific appearance of Jesus Christ, in 1820, to a young enquiring boy named Joseph Smith.[5] Joseph Smith, seeking to know which Christian church he should join, felt persuaded in his heart that he should pray and ask God,[6] just as the New Testament encourages in James 1:5-6, which states:

"If any of you lack wisdom, let him ask of God; Who giveth to all men liberally and upbraideth not, and it shall be given him. But let him ask in faith."

In answer to Joseph's prayer, God the Father and Jesus Christ appeared to the young boy[7] and instructed him to wait[8]—that the true church was not yet upon the earth,[9] but would be restored.

Modern Prophets proclaims that The Church of Jesus Christ of Latter-day Saints is the true[10] and full church[11] of Jesus Christ restored with apostles and prophets[12] to help gather Israel,[13] and prepare for the glorious and dreadful day of the return of Jesus Christ to the earth[14]—to rule in peace as its King of Kings[15] for a thousand-year millennium.[16]

Fulfillment of Prophecies of Messiah's 1st Coming

Modern Prophets states that Jesus Christ indeed is the promised Messiah[17] of the Torah and Book of Mormon. It affirms that He was born of the virgin Mary.[18]

One prophet, named Russell M. Nelson, spoke of Jesus Christ this way:

> "God the Father has given us the divine birth, the incomparable life, and the infinite atoning sacrifice of His Beloved Son, Jesus Christ."
>
> "He was the promised Messiah, the mortal Messiah, and will be the millennial Messiah."[19]

Another, Ulysses Soares, stated,

> "I testify to you that Jesus is the Christ, the Redeemer of the world, the promised Messiah, the Resurrection and the Life."[20]

And yet another, Russell M. Ballard, stated,

> "Christ is supreme. He is the righteous Judge, our faithful Advocate, our blessed Redeemer, the Good Shepherd, the promised Messiah, a true Friend."[21]

The Atonement of Jesus Christ

- ### Jesus Christ suffered for our Sins

One of the most pronounced teachings of Modern Prophets is that Jesus Christ suffered in the Garden of Gethsemane[22] and on the cross[23] for all the sins of mankind.[24]

Henry B. Eyring, states that,

> "The Savior paid the price of all sins, no matter how heinous."[25]

Further he states,

> "Jesus Christ bore in Gethsemane and on the cross the weight of all our sins."[26]

Dallin H. Oaks similarly teaches that,

> "Our Savior and Redeemer endured incomprehensible suffering to become a sacrifice for the sins of all mortals who would repent."[27]

And another prophet, Dieter F. Uchtdorf, explained,

> *"To find the most important day in history, we must go back to that evening almost 2,000 years ago in the Garden of Gethsemane when Jesus Christ knelt in intense prayer and offered Himself as a ransom for our sins. It was during this great and infinite sacrifice of unparalleled suffering in both body and spirit that Jesus Christ, even God, bled at every pore. Out of perfect love, He gave all that we might receive all."[28]*

- **Jesus Christ also suffered for our Pains and Afflictions**

In addition to suffering for sins, He also suffered for the pains and heartaches of every person ever to live upon the earth.

Russell M. Ballard taught that Christ,

> *"not only suffered for your sins" but…also suffered "pains and afflictions and temptations of every kind" so "that his bowels may be filled with mercy, according to the flesh, that he may know according to the flesh how to succor his people according to their infirmities…."[30]*

Ulysses Soares further explained,

> *"He personally experienced and took upon Himself in the flesh the pain of our weakness and infirmities."[29]*

Crucifixion and Death

Speaking of Jesus Christ's Crucifixion and death, these prophets state,

> *"Condescending to come to earth as the Only Begotten of the Father in the flesh, He was brutally reviled, mocked, spit upon, and scourged."*
>
> *"They mocked Him, placed a crown of thorns on His head, and clothed Him in a purple robe."*
>
> *"In Gethsemane, He trusted His Father, declaring, 'Nevertheless not my will, but thine, be done,' and then He exercised His agency to*

suffer for our sins. Through the humiliation of a public trial and the agony of crucifixion, He waited upon His Father, willing to be 'wounded for our transgressions ... [and] bruised for our iniquities.'"

Resurrection of Jesus Christ

At the very heart of the apostles' teachings is that Jesus Christ is alive today, having been resurrected from the dead and receiving a glorified body.

Joseph Smith and Sidney Rigdon record:

"And now after the many testimonies of Him which have been given, this is the testimony last of all which we give—that He lives! For we saw Him! And we heard the voice bearing record that by Him and through Him and of Him the worlds are and were created; and the inhabitants thereof are begotten sons and daughters unto God."

All of the following apostles bear witness that Jesus Christ is in fact resurrected and alive today:

Quentin L. Cook,
Ulysses Soares,
Joseph Smith,
Sidney Rigdon,
Boyd K. Packer,
Dale G. Renlund,
David A. Bednar,
Dieter F. Uchtdorf,
Henry B. Eyring,
M Russell Ballard,
Robert D. Hales,
Robert A. Rasband,
Russell M. Nelson,
Neil L. Andersen,

D. Todd Christofferson,
Thomas S. Monson,
Jeffrey R. Holland, and,
Gerrit W. Gong.

Some of their witnesses are particularly personal and sacred. For example, Boyd K. Packer said of Jesus Christ's resurrection:

> *"Joseph Smith and Sidney Rigdon recorded the following after a sacred experience:*
> *"'And now, after the many testimonies which have been given of him, this is the testimony, last of all, which we give of him: That he lives!*
> *"'For we saw him' (D&C 76:22-23)'*
> *"Their words are my words.*
> *"I believe and I am sure that Jesus is the Christ, the Son of God and that He lives."*

Teachings

Modern Prophets contains multiple teachings on topics, such as,

1) Who God is; that we are His offspring;
2) Where we lived before we were born;
3) Why we are here on this earth;
4) What does God expect us to do while here;
5) What happens when we die, and where we go;
6) How we can live together as husband and wife forever, with our families, if we so desire and qualify;
7) Why little children who die without baptism are saved anyway;
8) The valued position of women to God and throughout eternity; and,
9) Why we should make and keep covenants with God to return to Him.

Miracles

Modern Prophets does not sensationalize miracles, but it affirms that they are present in the Church today.

Russell M. Nelson said of miracles:

> *"Learn about miracles. Miracles come according to your faith in the Lord."*
>
> *"Seek and expect miracles. Moroni assured us that 'God has not ceased to be a God of miracles.' Every book of scripture demonstrates how willing the Lord is to intervene in the lives of those who believe in Him...*
>
> *"[T]he Lord will bless you with miracles if you believe in Him, 'doubting nothing.' Do the spiritual work to seek miracles. Prayerfully ask God to help you exercise that kind of faith."*

Establishment of the Church

Ten years following the appearance of God the Father and Jesus Christ to Joseph Smith (in 1820), divine messengers with authority were sent to Joseph Smith and Oliver Cowdery to restore the priesthood of God. Those messengers included John the Baptist (1829), Peter, James and John (1829), Moses, Elijah, and Elias (1836).

With that priesthood authority, in April 1830 the church of Jesus Christ was again formally organized on the earth.

Peter, James, and John ordained Joseph Smith and Oliver Cowdery as apostles in the Melchizedek Priesthood, and that holy apostleship has continued unbroken since then to the fifteen apostles so ordained today. Apostles in the church are also sustained as prophets.

Modern Prophets describes this restoration as follows:

> *"[The] Lord reestablished the Church of Jesus Christ once again through the Prophet Joseph Smith."*

"[W]e humbly declare that angels have returned to the earth in our day."

"God the Father and His Beloved Son, Jesus Christ, appeared to Joseph, a 14-year-old youth. That event marked the onset of the Restoration of the gospel of Jesus Christ in its fulness, precisely as foretold in the Holy Bible."

"Then came a succession of visits from heavenly messengers, including Moroni, John the Baptist, and the early Apostles Peter, James, and John. Others followed, including Moses, Elias, and Elijah. Each brought divine authority to bless God's children on the earth once again...."

"The keys and offices of the priesthood have been restored, including the offices of Apostle, Seventy, patriarch, high priest, elder, bishop, priest, teacher, and deacon.

Temples

Modern Prophets describes a temple practice which is certainly far more extensive than that described in other texts,

It begins with the doctrine that a temple is the house of the Lord, meaning the House of Jesus Christ where He could personally come and dwell should He choose. The existence of these temples is no longer unique, with new locations for the construction of new temples usually announced every six months.

The purpose of these temples is what makes these temples unique among Modern Prophets followers. Each temple has a four-fold purpose:

1) To serve as a place where faithful followers come and make solemn covenants of obedience and chastity as part of an ordinance;
2) To serve as a place where faithful followers come and become married or "sealed" to their spouse for their time upon earth and their eternity thereafter;

3) To serve as a place where faithful followers come and make similar covenants vicariously for their ancestors thus enabling them the opportunity to accept or reject such covenants. Primary among these ordinances "for the dead" is the covenant and ordinance of baptism, thus enabling all persons—living or dead—to be baptized should they so choose; and,
4) To serve as a place where faithful followers come and seek for peace and personal revelation to guide them in their family and life decisions.

Modern Prophets teaches that all people can talk to God in prayer and humbly seek His divine guidance for their lives. It teaches that such divine guidance comes through feelings in the heart and thoughts in the mind as "impressions" which the individual should then quickly follow.

Modern Prophets thus encourage the faithful to continuously repent and live pure lives so that they are able to enter these temples and participate in this covenant making and be strengthened thereafter to keep those covenants.

It also teaches that people should search for the names and identifying information of their ancestors (in a practice referred to as "family history") so that the temple covenant making and ordinances can be performed for such ancestors.

Gathering of Israel

Modern Prophets continues the teaching of the Torah, Book of Mormon, and New Testament that in the end days of the earth "Israel" will be gathered. This gathering seems to have at least two meanings:

1) They shall all be gathered together through baptism into one world-wide group of believers; and,
2) They shall at some point be restored to "lands of inheritance" which God has allocated to the faithful in different countries.

This gathering process is then synonymous with a world-wide missionary effort to proclaim the restoration of the gospel and The Church of Jesus Christ of Latter-day Saints throughout all the earth, among "every nation, kindred, tongue and people."

Because the temples provide the covenants and ordinance of baptism for deceased ancestors, this gathering effort is often times referred to as important on "both sides of the veil" of death. The gathering is thus encouraged among all the living, as well as among all the dead.

Recently one of the prophets, Rusell M. Nelson, declared that one of the key meanings of the word "Israel" is to refer to all persons of whatever race or lineage who are willing to "let God prevail" in their lives. Accordingly, the effort to "gather Israel" has much more to do with offering the covenant of baptism to all the living and all the dead than to bring together people who are actual descendants of Jacob, the grandson of Abraham.

Modern Prophets, does, however, advocate the gathering of the descendants of Jacob through baptism and their restoration to their lands of inheritance.

One such statement was provided by Joseph Smith in their famous Articles of Faith when he said:

"We believe in the literal gathering of Israel and in the restoration of the Ten Tribes; that Zion (the New Jerusalem) will be built upon the American continent, that Christ will reign personally upon the earth; and, that the earth will be renewed and receive its paradisiacal glory."

Prophecies of Messiah's Second Coming

Modern Prophets goes beyond the Torah, Book of Mormon, and New Testament in regards to the Messiah's glorious coming, or the Second Coming of Jesus Christ. These texts prophecy of such a future event when the "Son of Man" shall descend from the heavens with both the righteous who are then alive as well as the righteous who are then resurrected. Such event will be an act of judgment and destruction upon the wicked, and rescue and reward for the righteous. It will usher in the "Millenium" or thousand-year reign of Jesus Christ here upon the earth.

Modern Prophets goes beyond these prophecies of other texts in that it encourages all people now not only to look forward to such an event, but to take active steps to prepare for it.

Modern Prophets thus seeks to prepare the entire world for the pending return of Jesus Christ at His Second Coming.

Commandments

Modern Prophets encourages repentance and the keeping of the commandments. It teaches:

1) The importance of prayer;
2) Encouragement to study the word of God;
3) Being humble, meek, and lowly
4) Having faith in Jesus Christ;
5) Repenting of one's sins;
6) Being baptized by immersion by one having proper priesthood authority;
7) Following the Holy Ghost;
8) A husband being morally chaste and faithful to his wife;
9) The importance of men having just one wife;
10) The Ten Commandments;
11) Judging not;
12) Being charitable and giving to the beggar;
13) Serving other people;
14) Having hope; and,
15) Following the prophets.

In addition, Modern Prophets sets forth a health code for people, as was had among ancient Israel. The modern health code encourages the abstaining from tobacco and alcohol use, as well as moderation in other eating practices.

Sacrifice

Modern Prophets encourages the principle of sacrifice. It teaches, however, that the sacrificial offering of animals ended with the death of Jesus Christ whose body and blood were sacrificed as an atonement for the sins of all mankind.

The sacrifice encouraged by Modern Prophets may take several forms, but as a minimum includes a broken heart and a contrite spirit.

It also includes the subjecting of one's appetites, passions, and anger to a more pure and peaceful nature. It also includes the paying of "tithes and offerings."

Modern Prophets continues the teaching of Jesus Christ that mankind should "take upon themselves" the cross of Jesus Christ in the way of repelling lust and unhealthy appetites. It does not encourage the extinguishment of all appetites, but instead their harnessing for the good of the marriage, family, and society in general.

CHAPTER 7

The Sutra Pitakas (Limited)

The Sutra Pitakas (Limited)

The Sutra Pitakas, as one of three components of the TriPitakas, sets forth many of the teachings of Buddha. Among these teachings are the following:

- **Accountability**

An individual is not accountable for his feelings, thoughts, actions, or mental processes. This is because he is not the doer of any of these.[1] Because he makes no choice, he bears no responsibility for such choice.

- **Agency**

It is "not possible" that an individual determine his feelings, thoughts, actions, or mental processes.[2]

However, it does seem possible to follow an eight-fold path[3] and to discern many things.[4]

- **Birth**

Birth is painful.[5] We should live so as to be "released" and avoid rebirth ever again.[6]

- **Body**

The body is "aflame",[7] meaning it brings with it sensations and passions. Overcoming these passions is important to avoid suffering and to qualify to be "released."[8]

Otherwise, after death one is reborn again.

- **Buddha**

Buddha is not mentioned in the Sutras as a prophet, but a teacher.[9] A prophet receives revelation or communications from God. The Sutra Pitakas hardly speaks of God.[10]

Buddha teaches that the objective of life is to be "released."[11] He was released through his dispassion.[12] Consequently, there was no rebirth for him.[13]

- **Stressful, Inconstant**

The Sutra state that whatever is "inconstant" is stressful.[14] All of the following are inconstant:

1. body;[15]
2. consciousness;[16]
3. feelings;[17]
4. mental processes;[18] and
5. perceptions.[19]

- **Purpose of Life; Plan for Life**

The source or origin of life is not described. There is not a discussion of a spirit separate from one's body, mind, or feelings. However, there is the teaching that an individual "focus" on various things.[20] That focus seems to be directed by someone or something outside of one's body, mind, thoughts, or feelings.

The Sutra does not speak of a divine source or cause of life. Therefore, life may not have a purpose, but the objective of life is to be released from it through dispassion and detaching oneself from the world.[21]

A desire for "annihilation" in the present form of existence, however, is "heresy."[22] Many people who die will simply be reborn until they learn how through dispassion to become detached.[23]

- **God**

The Sutra speaks very little of God. In the Dhammakakkappavattana Sutra, it speaks of "gods in the highest heaven of heavens."[24]

- **Happiness**

The Sutra does not speak of a pursuit of happiness. Nor does it prescribe a course to find happiness.

To be sure, it speaks of becoming dispassionate regarding all emotions and feelings.[25]

The Sutra does speak of five monks who are "[g]lad at heart" and are "delighted" at the words of Buddha.[26]

- **Judging**

Judging others or not judging others does not seem to be defined as an issue in the Sutra, since the actions of one or another are "not mine…[t]his is not myself."[27]

Judging requires the supposition that one chooses his or her own actions, as well as his own action to judge another.

- **Light of Christ**

The Sutra does not reference the Light of Christ. Nor does it refer to Jesus Christ.

It does, however, in multiple passages in the Dhammakakkappavattana Sutra state that "within me...there arose the light."[28]

- **Love**

The Sutra does not speak of any importance or value of love. It does not encourage one "to love" or "to be loved." It does not seem according to the Sutras that any person has the ability to choose to love or not love.

Instead, the Anattalakkhana Sutra states "Any feeling whatsoever -- past, future, or present; internal or external; blatant or subtle; common or sublime; far or near: every feeling -- is to be seen as it actually is with right discernment as: 'This is not mine. This is not myself. This is not what I am.'"[29]

Rather than choosing to love, the Sutra encourages that one become "dispassionate"[30] and not be "attached."[31]

- **Lust**

The Sutra does speak of avoiding attachments.

But it also states that "every feeling" "is not mine", that it "is not myself", nor "what I am."

- **Pain & Suffering**

As with love and lust, pain and suffering—every feeling—"is not mine…is not myself", nor "what I am."

The Sutra Pitakas speaks often of pain. Among its many teachings are:

1. Birth is painful;
2. Death is painful;
3. Decay is painful;
4. Disease is painful;
5. Union with the unpleasant is painful;
6. Cravings that are unsatisfied are painful;
7. Pain results from existence as an individual. To be sure, most everything about our body causes us to be "aflame" with senses and passions.
8. For example, eyes and sight, ears and sounds, tongues and taste, noses and odors, the mind and mental consciousness are all "aflame" and as part of the body because they bring sensations and passions.

9. Therefore, in the Anattalakkhana Sutra, it states that a disciple should grow "disenchanted" with the body, become dispassionate, and then be "released."
10. It is not clear who, or what part of man, should choose to become disenchanted and dispassionate. Presumably it is not the body or mind itself.
11. Regarding the destruction of suffering, the Sutra states:
12. "Verily, it is the destruction, in which no passion remains, of this very thirst; the laying aside of, the getting rid of, the being free from, the harbouring no longer of this thirst.
13. "This then, O Bhikkhus, is the noble truth concerning the destruction of suffering."

- **Eight-Fold Path**

To achieve this destruction of suffering, the Sutra Pitakas teach an eight-fold path which includes all of the following:

a. Right aspirations;
b. Right conduct;
c. Right contemplation;
d. Right effort;
e. Right livelihood;
f. Right mindfulness;
g. Right speech; and,
h. Right views.

What part of self is capable and responsible for these choices is uncertain.

The Bhagavad Gita states that the soul is responsible for one's happiness. The Abrahamic texts indicate that the spirit in combination with the body make choices which bring happiness.

By comparison, the Sutra Pitakas state that "it is not possible (to say) with regard to mental processes, 'Let my mental processes be thus.'" It also states, that "it is not possible (to say) with regard to feeling, 'Let my feeling be thus.'"

- **Five Aggregates**

The Sutra Pitakas state that there are "five aggregates which spring from attachment (the conditions of individuality and their cause are painful…)."

- **These five aggregates are:**

1. body;
2. feelings;
3. perception;
4. mental processes; and,
5. consciousness.

- **Self**

The Sutra Pitakas state that all of the following are "not self":

Body;

Consciousness;

Feelings;

Mental Processes; and,

Perceptions.

- **Summary**

In summary, the Sutra Pitakas teach that we are not our body, thoughts, or feelings. It explains how the elements of our body—sight, hearing, taste, smell, and touch—bring passions. Unsatisfied passions or cravings are the source of suffering.

The Sutra Pitakas therefore encourage that we become dispassionate and detached from all sensations and desires.

Endnotes

Guidelines for MLA Endnotes are not followed here. Instead, the citation procedure is altered so as to maximize the quickness and clarity with which Endnotes create user understanding. Highlighting which religious text is being referenced in the citation is an important objective. Religious text names in some cases are slightly adjusted. In addition, the text name "Modern Prophets" is used to represent the combination of writings found in the *Doctrine & Covenants*, *Pearl of Great Price*, *Article of Faith*, and *Ensign* or *Liahona* general conference addresses of the First Presidency and Twelve from October, 2011 through the present. For brevity, initials of the speaker in such general conference addresses are used rather than their full name.

Expansive endnotes are enabled through modern use of technology.

Endnotes—Chapter 1, Torah, Nevi'im, and Ketuvim

[1] The Book of Mormon: Another Testament of Jesus Christ, Mosiah 12:34-36; The Book of Mormon: Another Testament of Jesus Christ, Mosiah 11:12-24; The Book of Mormon: Another Testament of Jesus Christ, 1 Nephi 4:2; 1 Nephi 5:11, 14-15; The Book of Mormon: Another Testament of Jesus Christ, 3 Nephi 12:21-33, 46

[2] The New Testament of Jesus Christ (KJV), John 5:47; The New Testament of Jesus Christ (KJV), Matthew 5:17-18, 21, 27, 31, 33, 38; The New Testament of Jesus Christ (KJV), Matthew 7:12; The New Testament of Jesus Christ (KJV), Luke 2:24; The New Testament of Jesus Christ (KJV), The New Testament of Jesus Christ (KJV), Luke 6:31; The New Testament of Jesus Christ (KJV), Galatians 3:24; The New Testament of Jesus Christ (KJV), Galatians 5:6; The New Testament of Jesus Christ (KJV), Romans 2:13, 15, 25, 29; The New Testament of Jesus Christ (KJV), Romans 3:20, 28, 31; The New Testament of Jesus Christ (KJV), Romans 9:31; The New Testament of Jesus Christ (KJV), Romans 10:4; The New Testament of Jesus Christ (KJV), Romans 13:8, 10; The New Testament of Jesus Christ (KJV), Hebrews 8:5; The New Testament of Jesus Christ (KJV), Hebrews 9:4-5, 8; The New Testament of Jesus Christ (KJV), Hebrews 10:1, 9, 11, 19

[3] The Holy Qur'an 3:50; The Holy Qur'an 4:136, 164; The Holy Qur'an 5:43-44, 46, 48, 66, 68, 110; The Holy Qur'an 11:110; The Holy Qur'an 17:2; The Holy Qur'an 23:49; The Holy Qur'an 25:35; The Holy Qur'an 28:43; 52; The Holy Qur'an 29:27; The Holy Qur'an 32:23; The Holy Qur'an 37:117-118; The Holy Qur'an 50:53-54; The Holy Qur'an 41:45; The Holy Qur'an 45:16; The Holy Qur'an 46:10; The Holy Qur'an 48:29; The Holy Qur'an 61:6; The Holy Qur'an 62:5; The Holy Qur'an 73:15; The Holy Qur'an 87:14

[4] Modern Prophets, Ensign, Nov 2011, TSM, 4, (8.33 Although); Modern Prophets, Ensign, May 2019, DAB, 5, (28.33 President); Modern Prophets, Ensign, May 2020, GWG, 3, (16.25 Let); Modern Prophets, Ensign, Nov 2020, DGR, 5, (7.24 When); Modern Prophets, Ensign, May, 2012, DHO, 1, (1.25 I); Modern Prophets, Ensign, Nov 2015, QLC, 1, (9.30 At); Modern Prophets, Ensign, Nov 2020, DGR, 5, (7.24 When)

[5] *The Torah*, Genesis 1:1-31; *The Torah*, Genesis 2:1-4

[6] *The Torah*, Genesis 1:26-31

[7] *The Torah*, Genesis 2:15-17; *The Torah*, Genesis 3:1-6

[8] *The Torah*, Genesis 3:8-24

[9] *The Torah*, Genesis 4:1-2, 25, *The Torah*, Genesis 5:4

[10] *The Torah*, Genesis 4:5-7

[11] *The Torah*, Genesis 4:8

[12] *The Torah*, Genesis 4:26-29

[13] *The Torah*, Genesis 15:5; *The Torah*, Genesis 17:2; *The Torah*, Genesis 18:10; *The Torah*, Genesis 22:17; *The Torah*, Genesis 26:4; *The Torah*, Genesis 28:14; *The Torah*, Exodus 4:26-2932:13; *The Torah*, Numbers 23:10; *The Torah*, Deuteronomy 28:11

[14] *The Torah*, Genesis 15:7, 18; *The Torah*, Genesis 17:8; *The Torah*, Genesis 28:4, 13, and 15; *The Torah*, Genesis 35:12; *The Torah*, Genesis 48:4; *The Torah*, Genesis 50:24; *The Torah*, Exodus 6:4; *The Torah*, Exodus 32:13; *The Torah*, Exodus 33:1; *The Torah*, Exodus 34:12

[15] *The Torah*, Genesis 17:19; *The Torah*, Genesis 22:9; *The Torah* 25:20; *The Torah*, Genesis 35:29

[16] *The Torah*, Genesis 25:25-34; *The Torah*, Genesis 29:23, 27, 30, 32-35; *The Torah*, Genesis 30:5, 7, 10, 12, 17, 19, 21, 23; *The Torah*, Genesis 33:4; *The Torah*, Genesis 35:10, 18, 23-26; *The Torah*,

Genesis 46:7, 15, 17; *The Torah,* Genesis 48:5; *The Torah,* Genesis 49:33; *The Torah,* Numbers 26:28

[17] *The Torah,* Genesis 22:1-2

[18] *The Torah,* Genesis 22:3

[19] *The Torah,* Genesis 22:7

[20] *The Torah,* Genesis 22:9

[21] *The Torah,* Genesis 22:11

[22] *The Torah,* Genesis 22:12

[23] *The Torah,* Genesis 22:13

[24] *The Torah,* Genesis 22:12

[25] *The Book of Mormon: Another Testament of Jesus Christ,* Jacob 4:5; *Modern Prophets, Pearl of Great Price, Moses 5:7*

[26] *The Torah,* Genesis 29:32-35; *The Torah,* Genesis 30:1-24; *The Torah,* Genesis 35:18, 24

[27] *The Torah,* Genesis 30:23-24

[28] *The Torah,* Genesis 37:5-11

[29] *The Torah,* Genesis 37:3

[30] *The Torah,* Genesis 37:4, 11-31

[31] *The Torah,* Genesis 37:32-36

[32] *The Torah,* Genesis 37:24-28, 36

[33] *The Torah,* Genesis 39:7-20

[34] *The Torah,* Genesis 39:21-23

[35] *The Torah,* Genesis 40:5-23

[36] *The Torah,* Genesis 41:1-37

[37] *The Torah,* Genesis 41:38-44

[38] *The Torah,* Genesis 41:47-57

[39] *The Torah,* Genesis 42:1-2

[40] *The Torah,* Genesis 42:3-5

[41] *The Torah,* Genesis 42:7-8

[42] *The Torah,* Genesis 42:9-26

[43] *The Torah,* Genesis 43:1-13

[44] *The Torah,* Genesis 43:25

[45] *The Torah,* Genesis 43:33

[46] *The Torah,* Genesis 43:34

[47] *The Torah,* Genesis 44:1-2

[48] *The Torah,* Genesis 44:3-17

[49] *The Torah,* Genesis 44:18-31

[50] *The Torah,* Genesis 44:32-34

[51] *The Torah,* Genesis 45:1

[52] *The Torah,* Genesis 45:1-4

[53] *The Torah,* Genesis 45:3

[54] *The Torah,* Genesis 45:5-15

[55] *The Torah,* Exodus 1:7-14

[56] *The Torah,* Exodus 3:7-10

[57] *The Torah,* Exodus 7:10-25, 8:1-32, 9:1-35, 10:1-29

[58] *The Torah,* Exodus 10:28

[59] *The Torah,* Exodus 11:1-10

[60] *The Torah,* Exodus 11:10

[61] *The Torah,* Exodus 12:29

⁶² *The Torah,* Exodus 12:1-13

⁶³ *The Torah,* Exodus 12:28

⁶⁴ *The Torah,* Exodus 12:14-27; *The Torah,* Exodus 28:16; *The Torah,* Deuteronomy 16:1

⁶⁵ *The New Testament of Jesus Christ (KJV),* John 1:29; *Modern Prophets, Ensign*, May 2020, GWG, 3, (16.25 Let, 17.25 Let); *Modern Prophets, Ensign*, May 2019, JRH, 2, (16.16 Beloved)

⁶⁶ *The Torah,* Exodus 12:30-33

⁶⁷ *The Torah,* Exodus 14:5-9

⁶⁸ *The Torah,* Exodus 14:10-12

⁶⁹ *The Torah,* Exodus 14:13-17

⁷⁰ *The Torah,* Exodus 14:21

⁷¹ *The Torah,* Exodus 14:21-22, 29-30

⁷² *The Torah,* Exodus 14:23-28; 15:6-12

⁷³ *The Torah,* Exodus 14:30

⁷⁴ *The Torah,* Exodus 19:1; 33:1-3

⁷⁵ *The Torah,* Exodus 19:1-3, 20

⁷⁶ *The Torah,* Exodus 19:18

⁷⁷ *The Torah,* Exodus 31:18

⁷⁸ *The Torah,* Exodus 32:19-20

⁷⁹ *The Torah,* Exodus 32:19

⁸⁰ *The Torah,* Exodus 34:1-2

⁸¹ *The Torah,* Exodus 20:1-17

⁸² *The Torah,* Exodus 20:1-17

[83] *The Torah,* Exodus 12:3, 5-7, 11, 13-18, 22.-23. 27. 31, 46, 13:4, 6-7, 23:15-16, 19, 34:18, 22, 26; *The Torah,* Leviticus 23:4, 6, 34; *The Torah,* Numbers 9:2, 5, 10, 13, 14, 28:16-18, 25, 29:12; *The Torah,* Deuteronomy 15:23, 16:1, 3, 8,, 10, 13, 15-16

[84] *The Torah,* Leviticus 23:27, 28, 36; *The Torah,* Numbers 28:26, 29:1

[85] *The Torah,* Deuteronomy 14:8

[86] *The Torah,* Genesis 9:4; *The Torah,* Leviticus 3:17, 7:26; *The Torah,* Deuteronomy 12:16, 23-24, 15:23

[87] *The Torah,* Deuteronomy 14:7; *The Torah,* Leviticus 11:4

[88] *The Torah,* Deuteronomy 14:7; *The Torah,* Leviticus 11:5

[89] *The Torah,* Leviticus 17:5, 22:8

[90] *The Torah,* Deuteronomy 14:19;

[91] *The Torah,* Deuteronomy 14:12;

[92] *The Torah,* Leviticus 11:13; *The Torah,* Deuteronomy 14:13

[93] *The Torah,* Deuteronomy 14:15

[94] *The Torah,* Deuteronomy 14:15-16

[95] *The Torah,* Leviticus 11:18

[96] *The Torah,* Deuteronomy 14:14; *The Torah,* Leviticus 11:15

[97] *The Torah,* Leviticus 11:29

[98] *The Torah,* Exodus 23:19

[99] *The Torah,* Numbers 19: 11, 14-16, 22, *The Torah,* Leviticus 5:2, 12:2, 13:45, 14:37, 41, 45, 15:2, 16, 18-19, 18:19, 22:4

[100] *The Torah,* Leviticus 15:19

[101] *The Torah,* Leviticus 13:50-59; *The Torah,* Numbers 19:16-19

[102] *The Ketuvim,* Psalm 96:13; *The Nevi'im,* Isaiah 2:19; *The Nevi'im,* Ezekiel 43:2

[103] *The Nevi'im,* Isaiah 10:17, 24:6, 66:15; *The Nevi'im,* Malachi 3:2, 4:1

[104] *The Ketuvim,* Psalm 9:8; *The Ketuvim,* Psalm 96:13; *The Nevi'im,* Isaiah 2:12

[105] *The Nevi'im,* Isaiah 10:17, 13:6, 9, 13, 19, 24:1, 6, 26:5, 66:15; *The Nevi'im,* Joel 1:15, 2:11; *The Nevi'im,* Malachi 3:2, 4:1

[106] *The Nevi'im,* Isaiah 26:5; *The Nevi'im,* Zechariah 14:4-5

[107] *The Nevi'im,* Isaiah 24:23; *The Nevi'im,* Zechariah 14:9

[108] *The Nevi'im,* Isaiah 7:14

[109] *The Nevi'im,* Isaiah 9:6

[110] *The Torah,* Numbers 24:17, 19; *The Nevi'im,* Micah 5:2

[111] *The Nevi'im,* Hosea 11:1

[112] *The Torah,* Deuteronomy 18:15-18

[113] *The Nevi'im,* Isaiah 53:2

[114] *The Nevi'im,* Isaiah 40:3

[115] *The Nevi'im,* Zechariah 9:9

[116] *The Ketuvim,* Psalm 41:9

[117] *The Nevi'im,* Zechariah 11:12

[118] *The Nevi'im,* Isaiah 53:5

[119] *The Nevi'im,* Isaiah 50:6

[120] *The Ketuvim,* Lamentations 3:30

[121] *The Nevi'im,* Isaiah 53:7

[122] *The Ketuvim,* Psalm 22:16; *The Nevi'im,* Zechariah 13:6

[123] *The Ketuvim,* Daniel 9:25-26

[124] *The Nevi'im,* Isaiah 53:9

[125] *The Ketuvim,* Psalm 22:18

[126] *The Nevi'im,* Zechariah 12:10-11, 13:6

[127] *The Nevi'im,* Zechariah 12:11

[128] *The New Testament of Jesus Christ (KJV),* Matthew 1:16-25

[129] *The New Testament of Jesus Christ (KJV),* Matthew 17:5, 22:44, 26:63; *The New Testament of Jesus Christ (KJV),* Mark 9:7; *The New Testament of Jesus Christ (KJV),* Luke 3:22, 1:35; *The New Testament of Jesus Christ (KJV),* John 1:14, 34, 9:37, 10:36, 11:27, 6:69; *The New Testament of Jesus Christ (KJV),* Romans 1:4; *The New Testament of Jesus Christ (KJV),* Colossians 1:15; *The New Testament of Jesus Christ (KJV),* Hebrews 1:5

[130] *The Book of Mormon: Another Testament of Jesus Christ,* 2 Nephi 12-27; *The Book of Mormon: Another Testament of Jesus Christ,* 1 Nephi 20-21; *The Book of Mormon: Another Testament of Jesus Christ,* Mosiah 12:27-37, 13:1-35; 14:1-12; *The Book of Mormon: Another Testament of Jesus Christ,* 3 Nephi 24-25

[131] *The Book of Mormon: Another Testament of Jesus Christ,* 1 Nephi 10:5-7, 9, 11, 11:24, 27, 31-34, 12:11, 13:40, 15:20, 19:9-10, 21:16, 22:20-21, 26; *The Book of Mormon: Another Testament of Jesus Christ,* 2 Nephi 2:7-9, 26-28, 9:6-7, 10, 12, 15, 21-22, 25-26, 41, 10:5, 25, 11:6-7, 12:19-20, 19:13, 23:8-9, 13, 15, 25:19, 26, 29, 26:3-4, 9, 24-25, 33, 31:13, 16, 19-20; *The Book of Mormon: Another Testament of Jesus Christ,* Jacob 1:8, 4:15-16; *The Book of Mormon: Another Testament of Jesus Christ,* Enos 1:27; *The Book of Mormon: Another Testament of Jesus Christ,* Omni 1:26; *The Book of Mormon: Another Testament of Jesus Christ,* Mosiah 3:6-11, 13, 15-16, 5:8, 13:33-35, 14:4-5, 7, 9, 11, 12, 15:2-3, 5-9, 11, 13-14, 19, 21, 23; 16:4, 6-9, 14, 15; *The Book of Mormon: Another Testament of Jesus Christ,* Alma 7:9-13, 9:26, 11:40, 42, 12:28, 22:14-15, 33:15, 19, 22, 34:6-10, 14-15, 37:37, 46-47, 42:15, 23; *The Book of Mormon: Another Testament of Jesus Christ,* Helaman 5:12, 8:15, 18, 20, 22, 14:3-5, 8, 12, 14, 16, 18, 20; *The Book of Mormon: Another Testament of Jesus Christ,* 3 Nephi 1:14-15, 19, 11:15

¹³² *The Book of Mormon: Another Testament of Jesus Christ,* Mosiah 3:8; *The Book of Mormon: Another Testament of Jesus Christ,* 2 Nephi 25:19; *The Book of Mormon: Another Testament of Jesus Christ,* 3 Nephi 11; *The Book of Mormon: Another Testament of Jesus Christ,* Alma 5:48, 36:17-20; *The Book of Mormon: Another Testament of Jesus Christ,* Mosiah 15:21; *The Book of Mormon: Another Testament of Jesus Christ,* Helaman 14:12

¹³³ *The Book of Mormon: Another Testament of Jesus Christ,* 1 Nephi 13:37, 22:15; *The Book of Mormon: Another Testament of Jesus Christ,* 2 Nephi 12:12, 19-20, 23:7-9, 13, 15, 26:4, 30:10; *The Book of Mormon: Another Testament of Jesus Christ,* Jacob 5:75, 6:3; *The Book of Mormon: Another Testament of Jesus Christ,* Alma 37:37; *The Book of Mormon: Another Testament of Jesus Christ,* 3 Nephi 25:1-3, 5; *The Book of Mormon: Another Testament of Jesus Christ,* Ether 4:19; *The Book of Mormon: Another Testament of Jesus Christ,* Moroni 7:48

¹³⁴ *The Torah,* Leviticus 17:11

¹³⁵ *The Torah,* Numbers 35:33

¹³⁶ *The Torah,* Leviticus 4:25

¹³⁷ *The Book of Mormon: Another Testament of Jesus Christ,* 3 Nephi 9:19-20, 15:4, 10; *The Book of Mormon: Another Testament of Jesus Christ,* Alma 34:13-14; *The Book of Mormon: Another Testament of Jesus Christ,* 4 Nephi 1:12; *The Book of Mormon: Another Testament of Jesus Christ,* Mosiah 3:15; *The New Testament of Jesus Christ (KJV),* Hebrews 9:22, 10:4, 12; *The New Testament of Jesus Christ (KJV),* Revelation 1:5, 12:11; *Modern Prophets, Ensign,* Nov 2012, BKP, 4, (28.31 That); *Modern Prophets, Ensign,* May 2019, DHO, 2, (9.21 We); *Modern Prophets, Liahona,* Nov 2021, DTC, 1, (10.22 Our)

¹³⁸ *The Nevi'im,* Isaiah 53:6

¹³⁹ *The Nevi'im,* Isaiah 53:11

¹⁴⁰ *The Nevi'im,* Isaiah 53:8

[141] *The Nevi'im,* Isaiah 63:9

[142] *The Nevi'im,* Isaiah 53:11

[143] *The Nevi'im,* Isaiah 53:5

[144] *The Nevi'im,* Zechariah 12:10

[145] *The Nevi'im,* Zechariah 13:6

[146] *The Nevi'im,* Zechariah 10:4

[147] *The Torah,* Exodus 12:46

[148] *The Nevi'im,* Zechariah 11:12

[149] *The Nevi'im,* Isaiah 26:19

[150] *The Nevi'im,* Ezekiel 37:6

[151] *The Nevi'im,* Hosea 13:14

[152] *The Nevi'im,* Isaiah 26:19

[153] *The Ketuvim,* Job 19:25-27

[154] *The Torah,* Genesis 1-3

[155] *The Torah,* Genesis 6-9

[156] *The Torah,* Genesis 19

[157] *The Torah,* Genesis 18:10-19, 21:1-8

[158] *The Torah,* Genesis 40-46

[159] *The Torah,* Exodus 7:14-25; 8:1-12:30

[160] *The Torah,* Exodus 12:1-31

[161] *The Torah,* Exodus 14:10-22

[162] *The Torah,* Exodus 14:19-20

[163] *The Torah,* Exodus 14:23-28

[164] *The Torah,* Numbers 16

[165] *The Torah*, Exodus 19-20

[166] *The Torah*, Exodus 24:9-10

[167] *The Torah*, Numbers 21:4-9

[168] *The Nevi'im*, Joshua 10:12-14

[169] *The Nevi'im*, 2 Kings 20:11; *The Nevi'im*, Isaiah 38:8

[170] *The Nevi'im*, Joshua 3:7-4:18

[171] *The Nevi'im*, 1 Kings 18:1-40

[172] *The Nevi'im*, 2 Kings 5:1-15

[173] *The Ketuvim*, Esther 3:1-8:8

[174] *The Nevi'im*, 2 Kings 6:6

[175] *The Nevi'im*, 2 Kings 7:6

[176] *The Nevi'im*, 2 Kings 19:32-35

[177] *The Nevi'im*, Joshua 6:1-21

[178] *The Nevi'im*, 2 Kings 4:1-7

[179] *The Nevi'im*, 2 Kings 4:18-37

[180] *The Nevi'im*, 1 Samuel 17:1-51

[181] *The Nevi'im*, 1 Kings 3:16-28

[182] *The Nevi'im*, 1 Samuel 1:1-20

[183] *The Ketuvim*, Daniel 2

[184] *The Ketuvim*, Daniel 3

[185] *The Ketuvim*, Daniel 6

[186] *The Torah*, Exodus 16:1-5

[187] *The Torah*, Exodus 17:1-6; *The Book of Mormon: Another Testament of Jesus Christ*, 2 Nephi 25:20; *The Holy Qur'an* 2:60

¹⁸⁸ *The Nevi'im,* 2 Kings 2:11

¹⁸⁹ *The Nevi'im,* 1 Kings 11:9

¹⁹⁰ *The Nevi'im,* Jonah 1:15-2:10

¹⁹¹ *The Torah,* Exodus 2:1-10

¹⁹² *The Nevi'im,* Joshua 1:2-11

¹⁹³ *The Nevi'im,* 1 Kings 17:1

¹⁹⁴ *The Nevi'im,* 2 Samuel 6:6; *The Nevi'im,* 1 Kings 12:33; *The Nevi'im,* 1 Kings 13:9; *The Ketuvim,* Psalm 106:43; *The Ketuvim,* 1 Chronicles 13:9; *The Book of Mormon: Another Testament of Jesus Christ,* Jacob 4:10; *Modern Prophets, Doctrine & Covenants, 22:4,,* 28:6, 85:8; *The Nevi'im,* 1 Kings 12:33; *The Nevi'im,* 1 Samuel 13:9; *The Torah,* Leviticus 17:4-5, 9, 10:1, 3:4, 26:61

¹⁹⁵ *Modern Prophets, Doctrine & Covenants 110:11*; *Modern Prophets, Ensign*, May 2018, QLC, 5, (4.33 One, 12.33 First); *Modern Prophets, Ensign*, May 2016, GES, 1, (6.24 Nearly); *Modern Prophets, Ensign*, May 2020, GWG, 3, (12.25 Following); *Modern Prophets, Liahona*, May 2022, QLC, 2, (20.25 After); *Modern Prophets, Ensign*, May 2020, HBE, 3, (9.22 It); *Modern Prophets, Ensign*, May 2013, RMN, 2, (14.21 Our)

¹⁹⁶ *Modern Prophets, Doctrine & Covenants 110:13-14*; *Modern Prophets, Ensign*, May 2018, QLC, 5, (4.33 One, 10.33 Third, 14.33 Third); *Modern Prophets, Ensign*, May 2016, GES, 1, (6.24 Nearly); *Modern Prophets, Ensign*, May 2020, GWG, 3, (12.25 Following, 13.25 The); *Modern Prophets, Ensign*, May 2017, HBE, 1, (15.32 Today); *Modern Prophets, Ensign*, May 2019, DTC, 4, (18.21 Also); *Modern Prophets, Liahona*, May 2021, HBE, 1, (18.29 We); *Modern Prophets, Ensign*, May 2016, QLC, 4, (3.55 On); *Modern Prophets, Ensign*, Nov 2011, DAB, 2, (6.28 Elijah, 7.28 Elijah); *Modern Prophets, Ensign*, May 2020, DAB, 4, (11.38 Elijah); *Modern Prophets, Ensign*, May 2016, QLC, 4, (3.35 On); *Modern Prophets, Liahona*, May 2021, RMN, 3, (10.27 Just);

[197] *Modern Prophets, Doctrine & Covenants* 110:12, 27:6-7; *Modern Prophets, Ensign*, May 2018, QLC, 5, (4.33 One, 9.33 Second, 13.33 Second); *Modern Prophets, Ensign*, May 2016, GES, 1, (6.24 Nearly); *Modern Prophets, Ensign*, May 2020, GWG, 3, (12.25 Following); *Modern Prophets, Liahona*, May 2013, RMN, 2, (14.21 Our)

[198] *The Torah,* Exodus 12:46

[199] *The Torah,* 1 Kings 5:5

[200] *The Nevi'im,* Micah 3:1;

[202] *The Torah,* 1 Kings 8:13; *The Torah,* 1 Kings 9:3

[203] *The Torah,* 1 Kings 1:50-51; 2:28

[204] *The Nevi'im,* Ezekiel 5:10, 12, 6:8, 7:16, 11:16, 20:23, 22:15, 39:23; *The Nevi'im,* Jeremiah 1:3, 5:10, 12, 6:8, 9:16, 13:19, 15;4, 16:13, 18:17, 20:4, 25:11, 26:21, 27:22, 37:8, 40:1, 41:11, 44:28, 52:4; *The Nevi'im,* 2 Kings 15:29, 17:6, 23, 18:11; 23:27, 24:10, 12, 14, 25:1, 7, 21, 25:26, 52:4; *The Nevi'im,* Isaiah 5:13, 7:8, 39:6; *The Nevi'im,* 1 Kings 9:7, 14:15; *The Nevi'im,* Zechariah 7:14; *The Torah,* Deuteronomy 4:27, 28:25, 64, 32:26; *The Ketuvim,* Daniel 9:2; *The Torah,* Nehemiah 1:8

[205] *The Nevi'im,* Jeremiah 3:18, 4:7, 7:5-6, 12:14-16, 16:15, 23:3, 7, 8, 29:14, 30:3, 31:7-8, 10, 32:37, 32:44, 46:16; *The Nevi'im,* Amos 9:11, 12, 14, 15; *The Nevi'im,* Zechariah 9:1, 16, 10:6, 8; *The Nevi'im,* Ezekiel 11:17, 20:34, 37, 41, 28:25, 34:13, 36:24, 37:14, 21-22, 39:25. 27, 28, 44:28; *The Nevi'im,* Isaiah 5, 29, 10:21, 11:10, 16, 14:1, 18:3, 51:11, 52:12, 54:7, 62:10; *The Nevi'im,* Amos 9:14; *The Nevi'im,* Micah 5:8; *The Torah,* Deuteronomy 30:3, 5; *The Torah,* Genesis 50:24; *The Torah,* Exodus 32:34; *The Ketuvim,* Psalm 14:7, 53:6, 107:3; *The Ketuvim,* Nehemiah 1:9, 7:6, 9:8; *The Ketuvim,* 2 Chronicles 28:11; *The Ketuvim,* 2 Chronicles 28:11

[206] *The Nevi'im,* Amos 9:12, 14-15; *The Torah,* Deuteronomy 30:5; *The Nevi'im,* Ezekiel 11:17, 36:24, 37:14, 221, 39:28, 44:28; *The Nevi'im,* Isaiah 14:1; *The Nevi'im,* Jeremiah 3:18, 7:5-6 12:14. 16:15. 23:3 8, 29:14, 30:3, 46:16; *The Ketuvim,* Nehemiah 9:8

[207] *The New Testament of Jesus Christ (KJV),* Romans 9:6, 8; *The New Testament of Jesus Christ (KJV),* Galatians 4:5; *Modern Prophets, Ensign,* May 2019, DTC, 4, (16.21 An); *Modern Prophets, Liahona,* May 2021, DTC, 5, (26.29 Scriptural); *Modern Prophets, Ensign,* Nov 2020, RMN, 4, (19.34 The, 10.34 This, 4.34 So); *Modern Prophets, Liahona,* Nov 2021, RMN, 1, (9.10 This); *The Book of Mormon: Another Testament of Jesus Christ,* 3 Nephi 5:25; *Modern Prophets, Ensign,* Nov 2019, RMN, 3, (20.32 We); *Modern Prophets, Liahona,* Nov 2021, DAB, 5, (17.32 Six)

[208] *The Book of Mormon: Another Testament of Jesus Christ,* 1 Nephi 22:11; *Modern Prophets, Liahona,* Nov 2013, QLC, 2, (12.28 The); *Modern Prophets, Doctrine & Covenants,* 45:9, 39:1; *The New Testament of Jesus Christ (KJV),* Galatians 4:5; *Modern Prophets, Ensign,* Nov 2020, RMN, 4, (19.34 The); *Modern Prophets, Ensign,* May 2019, DTC, 4, (16.21 An); *Modern Prophets, Liahona,* Nov 2021, RMN, 1, (9.10 This); *The Book of Mormon: Another Testament of Jesus Christ,* 2 Nephi 30:2

[209] *Modern Prophets, Ensign,* Nov 2020, RMN, 4, (19.34 The); *Modern Prophets, Ensign,* May 2019, DTC, 4, (16.21 An)

[210] *The Book of Mormon: Another Testament of Jesus Christ,* 2 Nephi 30:2; *The New Testament of Jesus Christ (KJV),* Romans 9:8; *The New Testament of Jesus Christ (KJV),* Galatians 4:5; *Modern Prophets, Ensign,* Nov 2020, RMN, 4, (19.34 The); *Modern Prophets, Ensign,* May 2019, DTC, 4, (16.21 An)

[211] *The New Testament of Jesus Christ (KJV),* Romans 9:6, 2:29

[212] *The Torah,* Exodus 20:3

[213] *The Torah,* Exodus 20:4

[214] *The Torah,* Exodus 20:5

[215] *The Torah,* Exodus 20:7

[216] *The Torah,* Exodus 20:8

[217] *The Torah,* Exodus 20:9

[218] *The Torah,* Exodus 20:10

[219] *The Torah,* Exodus 20:12

[220] *The Torah,* Exodus 20:13

[221] *The Torah,* Exodus 20:14

[222] *The Torah,* Exodus 20:15

[223] *The Torah,* Exodus 20:16

[224] *The Torah,* Exodus 20:17

[225] *The Torah,* Numbers 5:12-13

[226] *The Torah,* Exodus 21:22

[227] *The Torah,* Exodus 21:12-15, 18, 20

[228] *The Torah,* Exodus 21:15

[229] *The Torah,* Exodus 21:17

[230] *The Torah,* Exodus 22:19

[231] *The Torah,* Exodus 22:14-15

[232] *The Torah,* Leviticus 25:35-36

[233] *The Torah,* Exodus 22:22

[234] *The Torah,* Exodus 23:10

[235] *The Torah,* Exodus 22:29

[236] *The Torah,* Exodus 22:16

[237] *The Torah,* Exodus 22:28

[238] *The Torah,* Exodus 21:24

[239] *The Torah,* Exodus 21:16

[240] *The Torah,* Exodus 21:10

[241] *The Torah,* Exodus 21:33

[242] *The Torah*, Exodus 21:29, 28, 36, 35

[243] *The Torah*, Exodus 22:12

[244] *The Torah*, Exodus 23:4

[245] *The Torah*, Exodus 22:20

[246] *The Torah*, Exodus 22:21

[247] *The Torah*, Exodus 22:4, 7

[248] *The Ketuvim*, Ecclesiastes 12:13

[249] *The Torah*, Exodus 22:18

[250] *The Torah*, Leviticus 17:15, 22:8, 7:24; *The Torah*, Jeremiah 4:14; *The Torah*, Ezekiel 4:14, 44:31

[251] *The Torah*, Leviticus 11:2; *The Torah*, Deuteronomy 14:6

[252] *The Torah*, Deuteronomy 14:8

[253] *The Torah*, Deuteronomy 14:12; *The Torah*, Leviticus 11:13

[254] *The Torah*, Deuteronomy 14:14-15; *The Torah*, Leviticus 11:15

[255] *The Torah*, Deuteronomy 14:16

[256] *The Torah*, Exodus 23:19

[257] *The Torah*, Genesis 8:20, 22:2, 9; *The Torah*, Exodus 13:13, 35:5, 21, 29, 36:3; *The Torah*, Leviticus 10:1, 17:4-5, 9, 19:21, 20:2, 22:20, 23:12; *The Torah*, Numbers 3:4, 26:61; *The Torah*, Deuteronomy 12:31, 17:1; *The Nevi'im*, Judges 11:36, 39; *The Torah*, 1 Samuel 13:9, 15:22; *The Torah*, 2 Samuel 24:24; *The Torah*, 1 Kings 12:33; *The Ketuvim*, 1 Chronicles 21:22-24, 28:1, 3, 33:6; *The Torah*, Psalm 50:5, 51:17, 106:37-38; *The Nevi'im*, Jeremiah, 7:31, 19:5, 32:35; *The Nevi'im*, Ezekiel 16:20-21, 20:31, 22:37. 46:13; *The Nevi'im*, Hosea 6:6; *The Nevi'im*, Judges 11:36, 39; Malachi 1:13-14

[258] *The Torah*, Genesis 22:2

[259] *The Torah*, Genesis 22:3

[260] *The Torah*, Genesis 22:10

[261] *The Torah*, Genesis 22:11-12

[262] *The Torah*, Genesis 22:16-18

[263] *The Torah*, Genesis 22:17-18

[264] *The Book of Mormon: Another Testament of Jesus Christ*, Jacob 4:5; *Modern Prophets, Moses* 5:7

[265] *The Torah*, Exodus 29-30; *The Torah*, Leviticus 1-4, 6-7, 9-10, 14; 16:7, 22, 17:8, 19:5, 23:10; *The Torah*, Numbers 3:4. 5:15, 18, 8:11, 9:12, 18:11, 13, 19, 21, 24, 26, 28, 31, 19:2, 26:61, 28:3, 9-11, 29:20, 39; *The Torah*, Deuteronomy 12:6, 11, 26-27, 17:1; *The Nevi'im*, Joshua 13:14; *The Nevi'im*, 1 Samuel 13:9; *The Ketuvim*, 1 Chronicles 6:49; *The Ketuvim*, 2 Chronicles 32:12

[266] *The Nevi'im*, Ezekiel 40:38; 43-46; 13:14; *The Nevi'im*, Hosea 3:4, 6:6; *The Nevi'im*, Joel 1:9, 13; Malachi 1:7, 10; *The Ketuvim*, 1 Chronicles 16:40; *The Ketuvim*, 2 Chronicles 26:18, 29:27, 30:1

[267] *The Nevi'im*, Ezekiel 43:19, 22, 23, 25; 45:22, 25; *The Torah*, Leviticus 16:7, 22

[268] *The Torah*, Exodus 12:5; *The Torah*, Numbers 29:36, 19:2; *The Torah*, Deuteronomy 17:1; *The Nevi'im*, Ezekiel 46:6, 13

[269] *The Torah*, Numbers 3:4, 8:11; *The Ketuvim*, 2 Chronicles 26:18

[270] *The Ketuvim*, Psalm 34:18, 51:17; *The Nevi'im*, Isaiah 57:15; *The Book of Mormon: Another Testament of Jesus Christ*, 3 Nephi 9:20; *Modern Prophets, Ensign*, May 2012, DHO, 1, (3.25 The)

[271] *The Book of Mormon: Another Testament of Jesus Christ*, 2 Nephi 4:32; *The Book of Mormon: Another Testament of Jesus Christ*, Ether 4:15; *The Book of Mormon: Another Testament of Jesus Christ*, 3 Nephi 12:19, 9:20; *Modern Prophets, Ensign*, Nov 2013, DFU, 3, (19.36 Godly); *Modern Prophets, Ensign*, Nov 2013, DFU, 4, (24.48 Your); *Modern Prophets*, Doctrine & Covenants 59:8

Endnotes—Chapter 2, Shrimad Bhagavad Gita

All endnotes, except numbers 67 and 68, are to the https://www.holy-bhagavad-gita.org/ . Specific chapter and verse are indicated below:

[1] *The Shrimad Bhagavad Gita* 10:3

[2] *The Shrimad Bhagavad Gita* 4:10

[3] *The Shrimad Bhagavad Gita* 8:22

[4] *The Shrimad Bhagavad Gita* 8:13

[5] *The Shrimad Bhagavad Gita* 8:16

[6] *The Shrimad Bhagavad Gita* 14:27

[7] *The Shrimad Bhagavad Gita* 15:12

[8] *The Shrimad Bhagavad Gita* 12:3

[9] *The Shrimad Bhagavad Gita* 11:55

[10] *The Shrimad Bhagavad Gita* 18:61

[11] *The Shrimad Bhagavad Gita* 11:43

[12] *The Shrimad Bhagavad Gita* 9:4

[13] *The Shrimad Bhagavad Gita* 11:16

[14] *The Shrimad Bhagavad Gita* 11:39

[15] *The Shrimad Bhagavad Gita* 11:38

[16] *The Shrimad Bhagavad Gita* 10:31

[17] *The Shrimad Bhagavad Gita* 11:32

[18] *The Shrimad Bhagavad Gita* 10:38

[19] *The Shrimad Bhagavad Gita* 15:13

[20] *The Shrimad Bhagavad Gita* 4:5

[21] *The Shrimad Bhagavad Gita* 10:3

[22] *The Shrimad Bhagavad Gita* 15:8

[23] *The Shrimad Bhagavad Gita* 14:14

[24] *The Shrimad Bhagavad Gita* 14:15

[25] *The Shrimad Bhagavad Gita* 12:9

[26] *The Shrimad Bhagavad Gita* 12:9

[27] *The Shrimad Bhagavad Gita* 12:9

[28] *The Shrimad Bhagavad Gita* 2:64

[29] *The Shrimad Bhagavad Gita* 18:23

[30] *The Shrimad Bhagavad Gita* 18:26

[31] *The Shrimad Bhagavad Gita* 18:26

[32] *The Shrimad Bhagavad Gita* 18:26

[33] *The Shrimad Bhagavad Gita* 18:23

[34] *The Shrimad Bhagavad Gita* 18:9

[35] *The Shrimad Bhagavad Gita* 17:17

[36] *The Shrimad Bhagavad Gita* 17:20

[37] *The Shrimad Bhagavad Gita* 17:20

[38] *The Shrimad Bhagavad Gita* 18:33

[39] *The Shrimad Bhagavad Gita* 18:30

[40] *The Shrimad Bhagavad Gita* 18:30

[41] *The Shrimad Bhagavad Gita* 18:30

[42] *The Shrimad Bhagavad Gita* 18:42

[43] *The Shrimad Bhagavad Gita* 18:10

[44] *The Shrimad Bhagavad Gita* 18:24

[45] *The Shrimad Bhagavad Gita* 18:24

[46] *The Shrimad Bhagavad Gita* 18:27

[47] *The Shrimad Bhagavad Gita* 18:28

[48] *The Shrimad Bhagavad Gita* 18:25

[49] *The Shrimad Bhagavad Gita* 17:19

[50] *The Shrimad Bhagavad Gita* 17:22

[51] *The Shrimad Bhagavad Gita* 18:35

[52] *The Shrimad Bhagavad Gita* 18:39

[53] *The Shrimad Bhagavad Gita* 18:32

[54] *The Shrimad Bhagavad Gita* 18:22

[55] *The Shrimad Bhagavad Gita* 18:7

[56] *The Shrimad Bhagavad Gita* 12:18

[57] *The Shrimad Bhagavad Gita* 2:55

[58] *The Shrimad Bhagavad Gita* 12:16

[59] *The Shrimad Bhagavad Gita* 2:14

[61] *The Shrimad Bhagavad Gita* 4:10

[62] *The Shrimad Bhagavad Gita* 2:66

[63] *The Shrimad Bhagavad Gita* 12:6

[64] *The Shrimad Bhagavad Gita* 2:55

[65] *The Shrimad Bhagavad Gita* 4:23

[66] *The Shrimad Bhagavad Gita* 14:26

[67] *Isa Upanishad*, 1;

[68] *Isa Upanishad*, 1;

[69] *The Shrimad Bhagavad Gita* 4:39

[70] *The Shrimad Bhagavad Gita* 5:21

[71] *The Shrimad Bhagavad Gita* 4:10

[72] *The Shrimad Bhagavad Gita* 15:5

[73] *The Shrimad Bhagavad Gita* 13:13

[74] *The Shrimad Bhagavad Gita* 4:38

[75] *The Shrimad Bhagavad Gita* 4:39

[76] *The Shrimad Bhagavad Gita* 12:14

[77] *The Shrimad Bhagavad Gita* 8:8

[78] *The Shrimad Bhagavad Gita* 8:13

[79] *The Shrimad Bhagavad Gita* 8:5

[80] *The Shrimad Bhagavad Gita* 9:22

[81] *The Shrimad Bhagavad Gita* 9:15

[82] *The Shrimad Bhagavad Gita* 6:3

[83] *The Shrimad Bhagavad Gita* 6:12

[84] *The Shrimad Bhagavad Gita* 12:12

[85] *The Shrimad Bhagavad Gita* 18:41

[86] *The Shrimad Bhagavad Gita* 18:42

[87] *The Shrimad Bhagavad Gita* 18:43

[88] *The Shrimad Bhagavad Gita* 18:44

[89] *The Shrimad Bhagavad Gita* 18:44

[90] *The Shrimad Bhagavad Gita* 18:48

[91] *The Shrimad Bhagavad Gita* 18:47

[92] *The Shrimad Bhagavad Gita* 18:47

[93] *The Shrimad Bhagavad Gita* 18:46

[94] *The Shrimad Bhagavad Gita* 18:46

[95] *The Shrimad Bhagavad Gita* 18:61

[96] *The Shrimad Bhagavad Gita* 18:61

[97] *The Shrimad Bhagavad Gita* 13:30

[98] *The Shrimad Bhagavad Gita* 13:30

[99] *The Shrimad Bhagavad Gita* 3:27

[100] *The Shrimad Bhagavad Gita* 13:21

[101] *The Shrimad Bhagavad Gita* 15:8

[102] *The Shrimad Bhagavad Gita* 5:13

[103] *The Shrimad Bhagavad Gita* 18:33

[104] *The Shrimad Bhagavad Gita* 13:21

[105] *The Shrimad Bhagavad Gita* 13:9

[106] *The Shrimad Bhagavad Gita* 18:33

[107] *The Shrimad Bhagavad Gita* 14:15

[108] *The Shrimad Bhagavad Gita* 14:15

[109] *The Shrimad Bhagavad Gita* 5:17

[110] *The Shrimad Bhagavad Gita* 9:25

[111] *The Shrimad Bhagavad Gita* 9:20

[112] *The Shrimad Bhagavad Gita* 9:20

[113] *The Shrimad Bhagavad Gita* 9:21

[114] *The Shrimad Bhagavad Gita* 1:44

[115] *The Shrimad Bhagavad Gita* 16:16, and

[116] *The Shrimad Bhagavad Gita* 12:6

Endnotes—Chapter 3, The Book of Mormon: Another Testament of Christ

[1] *The Nevi'im,* Isaiah 24:23

[2] *The Nevi'im,* Isaiah 9:6

[3] *The Nevi'im,* Micah 5:2

[4] *The Nevi'im,* Isaiah 9:6

[5] *The Book of Mormon: Another Testament of Jesus Christ,* 1 Nephi 1:19, 10:4-7, 9, 11, 11:13, 24, 27, 31-34; 12:6, 11, 13:37, 40; 14:14, 15:13, 20, 17:41, 19:8-10, 20:2, 21:13, 16, 22:15, 20, 21, 26; *The Book of Mormon: Another Testament of Jesus Christ,* 2 Nephi 1:15, 2:4, 7-9, 26-28, 6:9, 7:6, 8:8, 9:5-7, 10, 12, 15, 21-22, 25-26, 41, 10:3, 5, 25, 11:3, 6-7, 12:12, 19-20, 16:3, 17:14, 18:14, 19:6, 13, 22:2, 23:7-9, 13, 15, 25:13, 19, 26, 29, 26:1, 3-4, 9, 24-25, 33, 30:10, 31:10, 13, 16, 19-20, 32:3, 33:10; *The Book of Mormon: Another Testament of Jesus Christ,* Jacob 1:7-8, 4:4, 15-16, 5:75, 6:3, 7:12; *The Book of Mormon: Another Testament of Jesus Christ,* Enos 1:6, 27; *The Book of Mormon: Another Testament of Jesus Christ,* Jarom 1:11; *The Book of Mormon: Another Testament of Jesus Christ,* Omni 1:25, 26; *The Book of Mormon: Another Testament of Jesus Christ,* Mosiah 3:5-11, 13, 15, 16, 5:2, 8, 7:33, 13:28, 33-35, 14:3-5, 7, 9, 11-12, 15:1-3, 5-9, 11, 13-14, 19, 21, 23, 16:2,4,6-9, 14-15, 18:10, 27:31; *The Book of Mormon: Another Testament of Jesus Christ,* Alma 5:33, 7:7, 9-13, 9:17, 26, 10:21, 11:39-40, 42, 12:15, 28, 13:26, 16:20, 19:13, 21:9, 22:10, 14-15, 18, 26:37, 27:27, 32:27, 33:11, 15, 19, 22, 34:2, 6-10, 14-15, 37:33, 37, 46-47, 38:9, 39:15, 40:3, 42:8, 15, 23, 45:16; *The Book of Mormon: Another Testament of Jesus Christ,* Helaman 3:28, 5:9, 12, 6:5, 8:14-15, 18, 20, 22, 13:6, 14:2-5, 8, 12, 14, 16, 18, 20; *The Book of Mormon: Another Testament of Jesus Christ,* 3 Nephi 1:9, 14-15, 19, 5:24, 8:20, 10:9, 11:8, 15

[6] *The Book of Mormon: Another Testament of Jesus Christ,* 2 Nephi 10:2-3

[7] *The Book of Mormon: Another Testament of Jesus Christ,* Mosiah 16:4-7

[8] *The Book of Mormon: Another Testament of Jesus Christ,* 1 Nephi 1:7, 2:1-4

[9] Fifty prophecies of the Messiah found in the Torah, Nevi'im, and Torah, are here listed together with the later New Testament fulfillment of each prophesy.

(#) Prophecy			
Fulfillment	Book	Chapter	Verse
(1) a virgin shall conceive	Isaiah	7	14
virgin shall be with child…bring forth a son…call his name Emmanuel…interpreted…God with us	Matthew	1	23
(2) thou, Bethlehem..though thou be little…out of thee shall he come forth…ruler in Israel	Micah	5	2
thou Bethlehem…art not the least among the princes of Juda…come a Governor…rule	Matthew	2	6
(3) in Ramah, lamentation, and bitter weeping; Rachel weeping for her children…they were not	Jeremiah	31	15
Herod...slew all the children that were in Bethlahem	Matthew	2	16
(4) I loved him, and called my son out of Egypt	Hosea	11	1
was there until the death of Herod…fulfilled which was spoken…Out of Egypt…called my son	Matthew	2	15
(5) come a Star out of Jacob	Numbers	24	17
Jesus Christ	Matthew	1	1

Abraham begat Isaac…begat Jacob…Judah…Phares	Matthew	1	2
(6) righteous Branch	Jeremiah	23	5
Jesus Christ	Matthew	1	1
(7) stem of Jesse	Isaiah	11	1
Jesus Christ	Matthew	1	1
Salmon begat Booz of Rachab…Booz begat Obed of Ruth…Obed begat Jesse	Matthew	1	5
And Jesse begat David the king; and David the king begat Solomon	Matthew	1	6
(8) The Lord thy God will raise up unto thee a Prophet from the midst…hearken	Deuteronomy	18	15
Prophet…like unto thee	Deuteronomy	18	18
The woman saith unto him, Sir, I perceive that thou art a prophet	John	4	19
(9) his name shall be called…Prince of Peace	Isaiah	9	6
let not your heart be troubled, neither let it be afraid	John	14	27
(10) voice of him…crieth in the wilderness, Prepare ye the way of the Lord, make straight	Isaiah	40	3
one crying in the wilderness, Prepare ye the way of the Lord, make his paths straight	Luke	3	4
writen in the prophets…I send my messenger…prepare thy way before thee	Mark	1	2
voice of one crying in the wilderness, Prepare ye the way of the Lord…paths straight	Mark	1	3
(11) To open the blind eyes, to bring out the prisoners from the prison	Isaiah	42	7

Behold my servant…beloved…put my spirit upon him…he shall shew judgment…Gentiles	Matthew	12	18
(12) I will open my mouth in a parable	Psalm	78	2
Watch ye therefore: for ye know not when the master of the house cometh	Mark	13	35
(13) neither was any deceit in his mouth	Isaiah	53	9
I am the way…truth…life: no man cometh unto the Father, but by me	John	14	6
(14) land of Zebulun…land of Naphtali…people walked in darkness have seen a great light	Isaiah	9	1
he came and dwelt in Capernaum…in the borders of Zabulon and Nephthalim	Matthew	4	13
might be fulfilled…Esaias…land of Zabulon…Nephthalim…people…saw great light	Matthew	4	14
The land of Zabulon, and the land of Nephtalim, by the way of the sea	Matthew	4	15
(15) walked in darkness…see a…light	Isaiah	9	2
The people which sat in darkness saw great light	Matthew	4	16
(16) Hear ye indeed, but understand not…see ye indeed, but perceive not	Isaiah	6	9
prophecy of Esaias…hearing ye shall hear…not understand…seeing…see…not perceive	Matthew	13	14
(17) he hath sent me to bind up the brokenhearted, to proclaim liberty to the captives	Isaiah	61	1

Neither do I condemn thee: go, and sin no more	John	8	11
(18) behold, thy King cometh unto thee	Zechariah	9	9
hosanna: Blessed is the King of Israel	John	12	13
Behold, thy King cometh unto thee, meek, and sitting upon an ass, and a colt	Matthew	21	5
they that followed, cried, saying, Hosanna; Blessed is he that cometh in the name…Lord	Mark	11	9
Blessed be the kingdom of our father David, that cometh in the name of the Lord: Hosanna	Mark	11	10
(19) riding upon an ass, and upon a colt	Zechariah	9	9
Jesus, when he had found a young ass, sat thereon	John	12	14
ass…colt…hosanna	Matthew	21	7
ye shall find a colt tied, whereon never man sat; loose him, and bring him	Mark	11	2
(20) precious corner stone	Isaiah	28	16
The stone which the builders rejected…same is become the head of the corner	Matthew	21	42
(21) stone…builders refused	Psalm	118	22
The stone which the builders rejected…same is become the head of the corner	Matthew	21	42
This is the stone which was set at nought of you builders…become…head…corner	Acts	4	11
(22) waves…thou stillest them	Psalm	89	9

peace, be still…wind ceased, and there was a great calm	Mark	4	39
(23) he maketh the storm a calm	Psalm	107	29
peace, be still…wind ceased, and there was a great calm	Mark	4	39
(24) Saviour…he bare them, and carried them all the days of old	Isaiah	63	9
his sweat was as it were great drops of blood falling down to the ground	Luke	22	44
(25) pleased the Lord to bruise him	Isaiah	53	10
shewed by…prophets…Christ should suffer, he hath so fulfilled	Acts	3	18
(26) for the transgression of my people was he stricken	Isaiah	53	8
his sweat was as it were great drops of blood falling down to the ground	Luke	22	44
(27) he was wounded for our transgressions	Isaiah	53	5
his sweat was as it were great drops of blood falling down to the ground	Luke	22	44
(28) Surely he hath borne our griefs, and carried our sorrow	Isaiah	53	4
Esaias…Himself took our infirmities, and bare our sicknesses	Matthew	8	17
(29) mine…friend…lifted up his heel	Psalm	41	9
Then one of the twelve, called Judas Iscariot, went unto the chief priests	Matthew	26	14
(30) sold the righteous for silver	Amos	2	6
thirty pieces of silver	Matthew	26	15
(31) So they weighed for my price thirty pieces of silver	Zechariah	11	12
(31) And I took the thirty pieces of silver, and cast them to the potter in the house of the Lord	Zechariah	11	13

fulfilled…Jeremy the prophet…they took the thirty pieces of silver, the price	Matthew	27	9
(32) They that hate me without a cause	Psalm	69	6
fulfilled that is written in their law, They hated me without a cause	John	15	25
(33) I was like a lamb or an ox that is brought to the slaughter	Jeremiah	11	19
Caiaphas	Matthew	26	57
(34) smite the shepherd, and the sheep shall be scattered	Zechariah	13	7
Then all the disciples forsook him	Matthew	26	56
And they all forsook him, and fled	Mark	14	50
be offended because of me this night..I will smite the shepherd…sheep…scattered	Matthew	14	27
be offended because of me this night…written…smite the shepherd…scattered	Matthew	26	31
(35) gave my back to the smiters	Isaiah	50	6
released he Barabbas unto them…scourged Jesus…delivered him to be crucified	Matthew	27	26
Pilate, willing to content the people, released Barabbas…Jesus..scourged him…crucified	Mark	15	15
Pilate therefore took Jesus, and scourged him	John	19	1
(36) he giveth his cheek	Lamentations	3	30
they spit in his face, and buffeted him…others smote him with the palms…hands	Matthew	26	67
(37) smiteth him	Lamentations	3	30

they spit in his face, and buffeted him…others smote him with the palms…hands	Matthew	26	67
(38) nail in his holy place	Ezra	9	8
(38) nail in a sure place	Isaiah	22	23
(38) out of him came forth…the nail	Zechariah	10	4
I shall see in his hands the print of the nails, and put my finger into the print of the nails	John	20	25
(39) they pierced my hands	Psalm	22	16
I shall see in his hands the print of the nails, and put my finger into the print of the nails	John	20	25
(40) he was numbered with the transgressors	Isaiah	53	12
scripture was fulfilled…he was numbered with the transgressors	Mark	15	28
(41) He trusted on the Lord that he would deliver him: let him deliver him	Psalm	22	8
Save thyself, and come down from the cross	Mark	15	30
Likewise also the chief priests mocking said…with the scribes…saved others; himself	Mark	15	31
(42) wag his head	Jeremiah	18	16
they that passed by railed on him, wagging their heads	Mark	15	29
Save thyself, and come down from the cross	Mark	15	30
(43) They gave me also gall for my meat; and in my thirst they gave me vinegar to drink	Psalm	69	21

one ran and filled a spunge full of vinegar, and put it on a reed, and gave him to drink	Mark	15	34
(44) my God, my God, why hast thou forsaken	Psalm	22	1
Jesus cried with a loud voice…"My God, my God, why hast thou forsaken me?"	Mark	15	36
(45) into thine hand I commit my spirit	Psalm	31	5
Father, into thy hands I commend my spirit	Luke	23	46
(46) they shall look upon me whom they have pierced	Zechariah	12	10
They shall look on him whom they pierced	John	19	37
(47) He keepeth all his bones: not one of them is broken	Psalm	69	21
scripture should be fulfilled, A bone of him shall not be broken	John	19	36
(48) They part my garments among them, and cast lots upon my vesture	Psalm	22	18
they parted his raiment, and cast lots	Luke	23	34
fulfilled…parted my garments among them…upon my vesture did they cast lots	Matthew	27	35
they had crucified him, they parted his garments, casting lots upon them	Mark	15	24
scripture might be fulfilled…They parted my raiment among them…my vesture…cast lots	John	19	24
(49) he made his grave with the wicked…neither was any deceit in his mouth	Isaiah	53	9

with him they crucify two thieves; the one on his right hand, and the other on his left	Mark	15	27
(50) Messiah be cut off	Daniel	9	26
Father, into thy hands I commend my spirit	Luke	23	46

[10] *The New Testament of Jesus Christ (KJV),* Luke 2:6-7

[11] *The New Testament of Jesus Christ (KJV),* Matthew 5-7, 11:29, 18:13, 4:17; *The New Testament of Jesus Christ (KJV),* Mark 1:22, 41, 10:18; *The New Testament of Jesus Christ (KJV),* Luke 5:32, 20:1; *The New Testament of Jesus Christ (KJV),* John 16:25, 8:29, 13:34

[12] (Faith in Jesus Christ:) *The New Testament of Jesus Christ (KJV),* Romans 9:30, 10:4, 9:32, 5:1, 10:17, 1:17, 3:28; *The New Testament of Jesus Christ (KJV),* Matthew 11:29, 28, 30; *The New Testament of Jesus Christ (KJV),* 1 Corinthians 15:19; *The New Testament of Jesus Christ (KJV),* Mark 13:6;

(Repentance:) *The New Testament of Jesus Christ (KJV),* Romans 5:1, 2:4; *The New Testament of Jesus Christ (KJV),* Revelation 2:16, 21, 22; Matthew 4:17, 6:15, 3:8, 3:2, 12:41, 11:20-21, 3:2, 12:41; *The New Testament of Jesus Christ (KJV),* Luke 3:3, 8, 15:7, 17, 3:3, 9; *The New Testament of Jesus Christ (KJV),* 1 John 1:9; *The New Testament of Jesus Christ (KJV),* Hebrews 12:1; *The New Testament of Jesus Christ (KJV),* Mark 9:45, 6:12; *The New Testament of Jesus Christ (KJV),* Acts 3:19, 26:20; *The New Testament of Jesus Christ (KJV),* 2 Corinthians 7:10, 5:17

(Baptism:) *The New Testament of Jesus Christ (KJV),* Acts 22:16, 8:36, 38, 19:5, 10:48, 4:4, 2:38, 41, 16:14, 33, 10:47; *The New Testament of Jesus Christ (KJV),* Galatians 6:2, 3:27; *The New Testament of Jesus Christ (KJV),* John 3:3, 5, 22, 23, 26; *The New Testament of Jesus Christ (KJV),* 1 Corinthians 1:16, 12:13; *The New Testament of Jesus Christ (KJV),* Colosians 2:12; *The New Testament of Jesus Christ (KJV),* Matthew 3:6, 8, 15-16, 28:19; *The New Testament of Jesus Christ (KJV),* Ephesians 4:5; *The New Testament of Jesus Christ (KJV),* 1 John 5:6; *The New Testament of Jesus Christ (KJV),* Mark 16:16; *The New Testament of Jesus Christ (KJV),* Luke 3:3, 7:30, 3:8; *The New Testament of Jesus Christ (KJV),* Romans 6:3, 4, 6

(Holy Ghost:) *The New Testament of Jesus Christ (KJV),* Acts 10:44-45, 11:16, 13:52, 8:17-18, 19:6, 19:2, 2:38, 7:51; *The New Testament of Jesus Christ (KJV),* John 16:13, 20:22, 14:16-17, 3:5; *The New Testament of Jesus Christ (KJV),* Mark 1:8; *The New Testament of Jesus Christ (KJV),* 2 Timothy 1:14; *The New Testament of Jesus Christ (KJV),* Galatians 5:16

[13] *The New Testament of Jesus Christ (KJV),* Matthew 1:21, 5:26, 9:6, 20:3, 5, 9, 26:28, 36-40, 42; *The New Testament of Jesus Christ (KJV),* Mark 2:10, 14:24, 32-34; *The New Testament of Jesus Christ (KJV),* Luke 4:18, 22:43, 44, 57; *The New Testament of Jesus Christ (KJV),* John 10:18, 12:32, 18:11, 19:17; *The New Testament of Jesus Christ (KJV),* Acts 5:31, 10:43, 17:3; *The New Testament of Jesus Christ (KJV),* Philippians 4:13; *The New Testament of Jesus Christ (KJV),* 1 John 1:7, 9; *The New Testament of Jesus Christ (KJV),* 1 Peter 2:24, 5:7; *The New Testament of Jesus Christ (KJV),* 1 Timothy 2:6; *The New Testament of Jesus Christ (KJV),* Hebrews 2:18, 4:15, 10:12; *The New Testament of Jesus Christ (KJV),* Revelation 1:5, 12:11

[14] *The New Testament of Jesus Christ (KJV),* Acts 5:31, 10:43; *The New Testament of Jesus Christ (KJV),* 1 Timothy 2:6; *The New Testament of Jesus Christ (KJV),* Matthew 9:6, 1:21; *The New Testament of Jesus Christ (KJV),* Mark 2:10; *The New Testament of Jesus Christ (KJV),* Hebrews 10:12; *The New Testament of Jesus Christ (KJV),* 1 Corinthians 15:3; *The New Testament of Jesus Christ (KJV),* John 12:32

[15] *The New Testament of Jesus Christ (KJV),* John 20; *The New Testament of Jesus Christ (KJV),* Luke 24; *The New Testament of Jesus Christ (KJV),* Mark 16; *The New Testament of Jesus Christ (KJV),* Matthew 28; *The New Testament of Jesus Christ (KJV),* John 21:1, 14; *The New Testament of Jesus Christ (KJV),* Acts 1:8, 11, 2:32, 4:33, 10:41, 13:31, 17:3, 22:15; *The New Testament of Jesus Christ (KJV),*

1 Corinthians 15:4, 6, 20, 22, 23, 55; *The New Testament of Jesus Christ (KJV),* Colossians 1:18; *The New Testament of Jesus Christ (KJV),* Matthew 12:40; *The New Testament of Jesus Christ (KJV),* Revelation 1:18, *The New Testament of Jesus Christ (KJV),* Romans 6:9

[16] *The New Testament of Jesus Christ (KJV),* John 20:1-17; *The New Testament of Jesus Christ (KJV),* 1 Corinthians 15:4

[17] *The Book of Mormon: Another Testament of Jesus Christ,* 3 Nephi 11:15

[18] *The Book of Mormon: Another Testament of Jesus Christ,* 3 Nephi 11-28

[19] *The Book of Mormon: Another Testament of Jesus Christ,* 3 Nephi 27:13, *The Book of Mormon: Another Testament of Jesus Christ,* Mormon 3:21, 7:5; *The Book of Mormon: Another Testament of Jesus Christ,* Moroni 7:34

[20] *The Book of Mormon: Another Testament of Jesus Christ,* 1 Nephi 10:6, 11:33, 12:11; *The Book of Mormon: Another Testament of Jesus Christ,* 2 Nephi 2:7, 27, 9:6-7, 10, 12, 21-22, 25-26, 10:25, 11:6, 25:26; *The Book of Mormon: Another Testament of Jesus Christ,* Jacob 7:12; *The Book of Mormon: Another Testament of Jesus Christ,* Enos 1:6; *The Book of Mormon: Another Testament of Jesus Christ,* Jarom 1:11; *The Book of Mormon: Another Testament of Jesus Christ,* Mosiah 3:7, 11, 13, 16, 13:28, 14:4-5, 11, 12, 15:8-9, 19, 16:4, 6, 15; *The Book of Mormon: Another Testament of Jesus Christ,* Alma 5:33, 7:11, 12, 13, 11:40, 12:15, 28, 21:9, 22:14, 33:22, 34:8-10, 14, 15, 39:15, 42:8, 15, 23; *The Book of Mormon: Another Testament of Jesus Christ,* Helaman 5:9, 8:18, 14:18; *The Book of Mormon: Another Testament of Jesus Christ,* 3 Nephi 11:11, 14; *The Book of Mormon: Another Testament of Jesus Christ,* Moroni 7:41, 8:19, 9:25, 10:33

[21] *The Book of Mormon: Another Testament of Jesus Christ,* Alma 22:14, 34:8, 42:15, 39:15; *The Book of Mormon: Another Testament of Jesus Christ,* 1 Nephi 11:33; *The Book of Mormon: Another Testament of Jesus Christ,* Mosiah 14:11, 15:9, 16:15

[22] *The Book of Mormon: Another Testament of Jesus Christ,* Mosiah 3:10; *The Book of Mormon: Another Testament of Jesus Christ,* 2 Nephi 2:8, 9:12, 15; *The Book of Mormon: Another Testament of Jesus Christ,* 3 Nephi 9:15; *The Book of Mormon: Another Testament of Jesus Christ,* Alma 7:12, 11:42, 22:14, 40:3; *The Book of Mormon: Another Testament of Jesus Christ,* Enos 1:6, 12:41; *The Book of Mormon: Another Testament of Jesus Christ,* Mosiah 15:8-9, 23, 16:7-8, 27:31; *The Book of Mormon: Another Testament of Jesus Christ,* Mormon 7:5-6, 9:12; *The Book of Mormon: Another Testament of Jesus Christ,* Moroni 7:41, 9:25

[23] *The Book of Mormon: Another Testament of Jesus Christ,* 3 Nephi 11:14-15, 17

[24] *The Book of Mormon: Another Testament of Jesus Christ,* 3 Nephi 11:1-2

[25] *The Book of Mormon: Another Testament of Jesus Christ,* 3 Nephi 11:10

[26] *The Book of Mormon: Another Testament of Jesus Christ,* 3 Nephi 11:15-17

[27] *The Book of Mormon: Another Testament of Jesus Christ,* 3 Nephi 11:14

[28] *The Book of Mormon: Another Testament of Jesus Christ,* Alma 7:9, 34:2; *The Book of Mormon: Another Testament of Jesus Christ,* 1 Nephi 13:40; *The Book of Mormon: Another Testament of Jesus Christ,* 3 Nephi 9:15

[29] *The Book of Mormon: Another Testament of Jesus Christ,* 2 Nephi 25:19; *The Book of Mormon: Another Testament of Jesus Christ,* Mosiah 3:8, 15:21; *The Book of Mormon: Another Testament of Jesus Christ,* Helaman 14:2, 12

[30] *The Book of Mormon: Another Testament of Jesus Christ,* Helaman 14:3-4

[31] *The Book of Mormon: Another Testament of Jesus Christ,* Helaman 14:4

[32] *The Book of Mormon: Another Testament of Jesus Christ,* 3 Nephi 11:1

[33] *The Book of Mormon: Another Testament of Jesus Christ,* 3 Nephi 8:5

[34] *The Book of Mormon: Another Testament of Jesus Christ,* 3 Nephi 11:7

[35] *The Book of Mormon: Another Testament of Jesus Christ,* 3 Nephi 11:8

[36] *The Book of Mormon: Another Testament of Jesus Christ,* 3 Nephi 11:10

[37] *The Book of Mormon: Another Testament of Jesus Christ,* 3 Nephi 11:14

believers and followers of Jesus Christ,[38] led by prophets,[39] who lived the law of Moses,[40]

[38] (People of Nephi, son of Lehi) *The Book of Mormon: Another Testament of Jesus Christ,* 2 Nephi 5:5-6; (People of Mosiah) *The Book of Mormon: Another Testament of Jesus Christ,* Mosiah 2:1-2; (People of Alma) *The Book of Mormon: Another Testament of Jesus Christ,* Alma 5:3; (People of Nephi, son of Nephi) *The Book of Mormon: Another Testament of Jesus Christ,* 3 Nephi 11:1-2

[39] (People of Nephi, son of Lehi) *The Book of Mormon: Another Testament of Jesus Christ,* 1 Nephi 10:17-22, 11-14; (People of Mosiah) *The Book of Mormon: Another Testament of Jesus Christ,* Mosiah 3:1-4; (People of Alma) *The Book of Mormon: Another Testament of Jesus Christ,* Alma 5:3; (People of Nephi, son of Nephi) *The Book of Mormon: Another Testament of Jesus Christ,* 3 Nephi 11:18-21

[40] (People of Nephi, son of Lehi) *The Book of Mormon: Another Testament of Jesus Christ* 2 Nephi 25:24; (People of Mosiah) *The Book*

of Mormon: Another Testament of Jesus Christ, Mosiah 2:3; (People of Alma) *The Book of Mormon: Another Testament of Jesus Christ,* Alma 34:13-14; (People of Nephi, son of Nephi—law of Moses fulfilled by Jesus Christ) *The Book of Mormon: Another Testament of Jesus Christ,* 3 Nephi 15:2-10

[41] *The Book of Mormon: Another Testament of Jesus Christ,* 3 Nephi 11-28

[42] *The Book of Mormon: Another Testament of Jesus Christ,* 1 Nephi 1:19, 10:4-5, 7, 9, 11, 11:13, 27, 31-33, 12:6, 13:37, 15:13, 20, 19:8-10, 21:16, 22:15, 20-21; 2 Nephi 2:8, 26, 6:9, 7:6, 10:3, 5, 11:7, 12:12, 19-20, 17:14, 19:6, 23:7-9, 13, 15, 25:13, 19, 26:1, 3-4, 9, 24, 30:10; 3 Nephi 1:9, 14-15, 5:24; Alma 7:7, 9-12, 9:26, 10:21, 13:26, 19:13, 33:15, 19, 34:8, 37:37, 45:16; Helaman 8:20, 13:6, 14:2-5, 12, 14, 16, 20; Jacob 4:4, 15, 5:75, 6:3; Jarom 1:11; Mosiah 3:5-10, 15, 33-35, 14:3, 5, 7, 9, 11, 15:1, 5-6, 9, 16:2

[43] *The Book of Mormon: Another Testament of Jesus Christ,* 1 Nephi 1:4

[44] *The Book of Mormon: Another Testament of Jesus Christ,* Mormon 8:6

[45] *The Book of Mormon: Another Testament of Jesus Christ,* 2 Nephi 2:6-8

[46] *The Book of Mormon: Another Testament of Jesus Christ,* Mosiah 13:33-35

[47] *The Book of Mormon: Another Testament of Jesus Christ,* Alma 7:9, 34:2; *The Book of Mormon: Another Testament of Jesus Christ,* 1 Nephi 13:40; *The Book of Mormon: Another Testament of Jesus Christ,* 3 Nephi 9:15; *The Book of Mormon: Another Testament of Jesus Christ,* 2 Nephi 25:19; *The Book of Mormon: Another Testament of Jesus Christ,* Mosiah 3:8, 15:21; *The Book of Mormon: Another Testament of Jesus Christ,* Helaman 14:2, 12

[48] *The Book of Mormon: Another Testament of Jesus Christ,* Mosiah 3:5, 7

⁴⁹ *The Book of Mormon: Another Testament of Jesus Christ,* Helaman 14:4

⁵⁰ *The Book of Mormon: Another Testament of Jesus Christ,* 3 Nephi 1:5-7

⁵¹ *The Book of Mormon: Another Testament of Jesus Christ,* 3 Nephi 1:9

⁵² *The Book of Mormon: Another Testament of Jesus Christ,* 3 Nephi 1:10

⁵³ *The Book of Mormon: Another Testament of Jesus Christ,* 3 Nephi 1:11

⁵⁴ *The Book of Mormon: Another Testament of Jesus Christ,* 3 Nephi 1:15

⁵⁵ *The Book of Mormon: Another Testament of Jesus Christ,* 3 Nephi 1:16

⁵⁶ *The Book of Mormon: Another Testament of Jesus Christ,* Mosiah 3:7

⁵⁷ *The Book of Mormon: Another Testament of Jesus Christ, Mosiah 3:12; The Book of Mormon: Another Testament of Jesus Christ,* Alma 34:16; *The Book of Mormon: Another Testament of Jesus Christ,* Moroni 10:26; *The Book of Mormon: Another Testament of Jesus Christ,* Alma 42:24; *The Book of Mormon: Another Testament of Jesus Christ,* Helaman 12:23; *The Book of Mormon: Another Testament of Jesus Christ,* 3 Nephi 11:38; *The Book of Mormon: Another Testament of Jesus Christ,* Alma 34:37; *The Book of Mormon: Another Testament of Jesus Christ,* 2 Nephi 2:7, 21, 9:16, 23-24, 46, 28:8; *The Book of Mormon: Another Testament of Jesus Christ,* Mosiah 4:8, 10, 15:26, 16:4-5, 12, 27:25; *The Book of Mormon: Another Testament of Jesus Christ,* Alma 1:4, 3:27, 5:13, 21, 25, 31, 51, 9:12, 11:34, 37, 41, 12:26, 21:6, 22:6, 37:25, 26, 42:3, 5, 13; *The Book of Mormon: Another Testament of Jesus Christ,* Helaman 14:18-19; *The Book of Mormon: Another Testament of Jesus Christ,* 3 Nephi 11:32, 12:19, 28:34; *The Book of Mormon: Another Testament of Jesus Christ,* Mormon 9:3-4;

The Book of Mormon: Another Testament of Jesus Christ, Moroni 7:34, 8:10, 19, 9:26

[58] *The Book of Mormon: Another Testament of Jesus Christ,* Alma 34:15-17

[59] *The Book of Mormon: Another Testament of Jesus Christ,* Mosiah 4:10, 26:29, 35, 27:35; *The Book of Mormon: Another Testament of Jesus Christ,* Alma 39:9, 13, 13:16, 22:18, 24:12, 16, 19, 23, 27:3; *The Book of Mormon: Another Testament of Jesus Christ,* 3 Nephi 13:14, 5:3; *The Book of Mormon: Another Testament of Jesus Christ,* Ether 2:15

[60] *The Book of Mormon: Another Testament of Jesus Christ,* Mosiah 26:30, 4:3; *The Book of Mormon: Another Testament of Jesus Christ,* Alma 36:21, 34:31, 36:19-20; *The Book of Mormon: Another Testament of Jesus Christ,* Enos 1:6; *The Book of Mormon: Another Testament of Jesus Christ,* 2 Nephi 9:46

[61] *The Book of Mormon: Another Testament of Jesus Christ,* Mosiah 5:7, 27:25, 5:2; *The Book of Mormon: Another Testament of Jesus Christ,* Alma 19:33, 5:49, 7:14

[62] *The Book of Mormon: Another Testament of Jesus Christ,* Mosiah 5:2, 27:25, 18:9; *The Book of Mormon: Another Testament of Jesus Christ,* 2 Nephi 9:23, 31:5, 13; *The Book of Mormon: Another Testament of Jesus Christ,* Mormon 9:23; *The Book of Mormon: Another Testament of Jesus Christ,* Ether 4:18; *The Book of Mormon: Another Testament of Jesus Christ,* Moroni 8:10-11, 7:34

[63] *The Book of Mormon: Another Testament of Jesus Christ,* 2 Nephi 31:13; *The Book of Mormon: Another Testament of Jesus Christ,* Mosiah 5:2; *The Book of Mormon: Another Testament of Jesus Christ,* Alma 19:33

[64] *The Book of Mormon: Another Testament of Jesus Christ,* 3 Nephi 8:5

[65] *The Book of Mormon: Another Testament of Jesus Christ,* 3 Nephi 8-9, 10:12-13

[66] *The Book of Mormon: Another Testament of Jesus Christ,* 3 Nephi 10:12-13

[67] *The Book of Mormon: Another Testament of Jesus Christ,* 3 Nephi 8:8, 14

[68] *The Book of Mormon: Another Testament of Jesus Christ,* 3 Nephi 8:10

[69] *The Book of Mormon: Another Testament of Jesus Christ,* 3 Nephi 8:10, 14

[70] *The Book of Mormon: Another Testament of Jesus Christ,* 3 Nephi 11:1-26:13

[71] *The Book of Mormon: Another Testament of Jesus Christ,* 3 Nephi 26:13, 27:2

[72] *The Book of Mormon: Another Testament of Jesus Christ,* 1 Nephi 20-21; 2 Nephi 12-24, 27

[73] *The Book of Mormon: Another Testament of Jesus Christ,* Alma 7:9, 34:2; *The Book of Mormon: Another Testament of Jesus Christ,* 1 Nephi 13:40; *The Book of Mormon: Another Testament of Jesus Christ,* 3 Nephi 9:15; *The Book of Mormon: Another Testament of Jesus Christ,* 2 Nephi 25:19; *The Book of Mormon: Another Testament of Jesus Christ,* Mosiah 3:8, 15:21; *The Book of Mormon: Another Testament of Jesus Christ,* Helaman 14:2, 12

[74] *The Book of Mormon: Another Testament of Jesus Christ,* Ether 6:4: *The Book of Mormon: Another Testament of Jesus Christ,* Moroni 8:16; *The Book of Mormon: Another Testament of Jesus Christ,* 2 Nephi 4:34, 28:31; *The Book of Mormon: Another Testament of Jesus Christ,* Mosiah 7:33, 23:22, 29:20, 24:14-15,7:19; *The Book of Mormon: Another Testament of Jesus Christ,* Alma 61:13, 5:13, 38:5, 58:33, 37; *The Book of Mormon: Another Testament of Jesus Christ,* Helaman 12:1

[75] *The Book of Mormon: Another Testament of Jesus Christ, Mosiah 3:12; The Book of Mormon: Another Testament of Jesus Christ,* Alma

34:16; *The Book of Mormon: Another Testament of Jesus Christ,* Moroni 10:26; *The Book of Mormon: Another Testament of Jesus Christ,* Alma 42:24; *The Book of Mormon: Another Testament of Jesus Christ,* Helaman 12:23; *The Book of Mormon: Another Testament of Jesus Christ,* 3 Nephi 11:38; *The Book of Mormon: Another Testament of Jesus Christ,* Alma 34:37; *The Book of Mormon: Another Testament of Jesus Christ,* 2 Nephi 2:7, 21, 9:16, 23-24, 46, 28:8; *The Book of Mormon: Another Testament of Jesus Christ,* Mosiah 4:8, 10, 15:26, 16:4-5, 12, 27:25; *The Book of Mormon: Another Testament of Jesus Christ,* Alma 1:4, 3:27, 5:13, 21, 25, 31, 51, 9:12, 11:34, 37, 41, 12:26, 21:6, 22:6, 37:25, 26, 42:3, 5, 13; *The Book of Mormon: Another Testament of Jesus Christ,* Helaman 14:18-19; *The Book of Mormon: Another Testament of Jesus Christ,* 3 Nephi 11:32, 12:19, 28:34; *The Book of Mormon: Another Testament of Jesus Christ,* Mormon 9:3-4; *The Book of Mormon: Another Testament of Jesus Christ,* Moroni 7:34, 8:10, 19, 9:26

[76] *The Book of Mormon: Another Testament of Jesus Christ,* 2 Nephi 4:24; *The Book of Mormon: Another Testament of Jesus Christ,* Alma 24:14, 40:11; *The Book of Mormon: Another Testament of Jesus Christ,* Jacob 7:5; *The Book of Mormon: Another Testament of Jesus Christ,* Mosiah 3:2; *The Book of Mormon: Another Testament of Jesus Christ,* 3 Nephi 7:15

[77] *The Book of Mormon: Another Testament of Jesus Christ,* Alma 27:27; *The Book of Mormon: Another Testament of Jesus Christ,* 2 Nephi 31:19; *The Book of Mormon: Another Testament of Jesus Christ,* Alma 32:27; *The Book of Mormon: Another Testament of Jesus Christ,* 1 Nephi 12:11; *The Book of Mormon: Another Testament of Jesus Christ,* Helaman 8:15; *The Book of Mormon: Another Testament of Jesus Christ,* Mosiah 4:3; *The Book of Mormon: Another Testament of Jesus Christ,* Alma 33:22, 37:33, 34:17; *The Book of Mormon: Another Testament of Jesus Christ,* Mosiah 24:15; *The Book of Mormon: Another Testament of Jesus Christ,* Helaman 3:28; *The Book of Mormon: Another Testament of Jesus Christ,* 1 Nephi 12:11

[78] *The Book of Mormon: Another Testament of Jesus Christ, Mosiah 3:12; The Book of Mormon: Another Testament of Jesus Christ,* Alma

34:15-17; *The Book of Mormon: Another Testament of Jesus Christ,* Moroni 10:26; *The Book of Mormon: Another Testament of Jesus Christ,* Alma 42:24; *The Book of Mormon: Another Testament of Jesus Christ,* Helaman 12:23; *The Book of Mormon: Another Testament of Jesus Christ,* 3 Nephi 11:38; *The Book of Mormon: Another Testament of Jesus Christ,* Alma 34:37; *The Book of Mormon: Another Testament of Jesus Christ,* 2 Nephi 2:7, 21, 9:16, 23-24, 46, 28:8; *The Book of Mormon: Another Testament of Jesus Christ,* Mosiah 4:8, 10, 15:26, 16:4-5, 12, 27:25; *The Book of Mormon: Another Testament of Jesus Christ,* Alma 1:4, 3:27, 5:13, 21, 25, 31, 51, 9:12, 11:34, 37, 41, 12:26, 21:6, 22:6, 37:25, 26, 42:3, 5, 13; *The Book of Mormon: Another Testament of Jesus Christ,* Helaman 14:18-19; *The Book of Mormon: Another Testament of Jesus Christ,* 3 Nephi 11:32, 12:19, 28:34; *The Book of Mormon: Another Testament of Jesus Christ,* Mormon 9:3-4; *The Book of Mormon: Another Testament of Jesus Christ,* Moroni 7:34, 8:10, 19, 9:26

[79] *The Book of Mormon: Another Testament of Jesus Christ,* Moroni 11:27; *The Book of Mormon: Another Testament of Jesus Christ,* 2 Nephi 31:12, 18, 17, 7, 10, 13; 31:5, 13; *The Book of Mormon: Another Testament of Jesus Christ,* Mosiah 21:33, 18:10, 8-9, 13, 10, 15-16, 5:2, 27:25, *The Book of Mormon: Another Testament of Jesus Christ,* Alma 7:14-15, 4:4-5, 26:4, 23:5, 26:22, 13, 5:60; *The Book of Mormon: Another Testament of Jesus Christ,* Helaman 5:19, 3:26, 24, 16:5, 1, 4; *The Book of Mormon: Another Testament of Jesus Christ,* 3 Nephi 11:21-22, 25, 26:16, 30:2, 12:1-2, 1:23, 22:10, 7:25, 26:17, 28:18, 11:26, 7:24, 11:24-25, 34, 28:23, 27:20, 11:23; *The Book of Mormon: Another Testament of Jesus Christ,* 4 Nephi 1:1-2; *The Book of Mormon: Another Testament of Jesus Christ,* Mormon 7:7-8, 9:23, 29; *The Book of Mormon: Another Testament of Jesus Christ,* Ether 4:18; *The Book of Mormon: Another Testament of Jesus Christ,* Moroni 8:10-11, 15, 14, 19, 21, 9, 6:1-3, 8:25, 7:34

[80] *The Book of Mormon: Another Testament of Jesus Christ,* 1 Nephi 4:6; *The Book of Mormon: Another Testament of Jesus Christ,* 2 Nephi 31:13, 32:5; *The Book of Mormon: Another Testament of Jesus Christ,* Mosiah 3:19; *The Book of Mormon: Another Testament of Jesus Christ,*

Alma 34:38, 21:16; *The Book of Mormon: Another Testament of Jesus Christ,* Helaman 5:45; *The Book of Mormon: Another Testament of Jesus Christ,* Moroni 6:9

[81] *The Book of Mormon: Another Testament of Jesus Christ,* Moroni 10:4-5; *The Book of Mormon: Another Testament of Jesus Christ,* Alma 32:27, 17:2; *The Book of Mormon: Another Testament of Jesus Christ,* Helaman 7:29; *The Book of Mormon: Another Testament of Jesus Christ,* Mosiah 5:2, 27:14; *The Book of Mormon: Another Testament of Jesus Christ,* Moroni 7:19, 16, 10:3; *The Book of Mormon: Another Testament of Jesus Christ,* 2 Nephi 2:5; *The Book of Mormon: Another Testament of Jesus Christ,* 3 Nephi 7:18; *The Book of Mormon: Another Testament of Jesus Christ,* Ether 8:26

[82] *The Book of Mormon: Another Testament of Jesus Christ,* 3 Nephi 12:3-14:27

[83] *The Book of Mormon: Another Testament of Jesus Christ,* 3 Nephi 12:7

[84] *The Book of Mormon: Another Testament of Jesus Christ,* 3 Nephi 12:9

[85] *The Book of Mormon: Another Testament of Jesus Christ,* 3 Nephi 14:1-5

[86] *The Book of Mormon: Another Testament of Jesus Christ,* 3 Nephi 14:7-12

[87] *The Book of Mormon: Another Testament of Jesus Christ,* 2 Nephi 27:23, 25:20; *The Book of Mormon: Another Testament of Jesus Christ,* Mosiah 8:18; *The Book of Mormon: Another Testament of Jesus Christ,* Alma 37:41; *The Book of Mormon: Another Testament of Jesus Christ,* Helaman 16:2; *The Book of Mormon: Another Testament of Jesus Christ,* 3 Nephi 8:1, 7:19; 4 *The Book of Mormon: Another Testament of Jesus Christ,* Nephi 1:5, 13, 30; *The Book of Mormon: Another Testament of Jesus Christ,* Mormon 9:24, *The Book of Mormon: Another Testament of Jesus Christ,* Ether 12:12; *The Book of Mormon: Another Testament of Jesus Christ,* Moroni 10:7; *The Book of Mormon: Another Testament of Jesus Christ,* 2 Nephi 28:5; *The*

Book of Mormon: Another Testament of Jesus Christ, 3 Nephi 19:35; *The Book of Mormon: Another Testament of Jesus Christ,* Ether 12:30; *The Book of Mormon: Another Testament of Jesus Christ,* Moroni 7:37, 27, 29, 10:7

[88] *The Book of Mormon: Another Testament of Jesus Christ,* 1 Nephi 18:12-15, 20-22

[89] *The Book of Mormon: Another Testament of Jesus Christ,* 1 Nephi 1:9-10

[90] *The Book of Mormon: Another Testament of Jesus Christ,* Helaman 8:27-28; 9

[91] *The Book of Mormon: Another Testament of Jesus Christ,* 3 Nephi 26:15

[92] *The Book of Mormon: Another Testament of Jesus Christ,* 3 Nephi 17:11-18

[93] *The Book of Mormon: Another Testament of Jesus Christ,* 3 Nephi 17:24-25

[94] *The Book of Mormon: Another Testament of Jesus Christ,* Helaman 5:21-50; *The Book of Mormon: Another Testament of Jesus Christ,* Alma 20:3-5, 28, 21:13-15

[95] *The Book of Mormon: Another Testament of Jesus Christ,* Alma 56:1-56; 57:12-26

[96] *The Book of Mormon: Another Testament of Jesus Christ,* 3 Nephi 7:17-18

[97] *The Book of Mormon: Another Testament of Jesus Christ,* Jacob 1:18; *The Book of Mormon: Another Testament of Jesus Christ,* Moroni 3:1-4; *The Book of Mormon: Another Testament of Jesus Christ,* Alma 6:1

[98] *The Book of Mormon: Another Testament of Jesus Christ,* Moroni 3:3

[99] *The Book of Mormon: Another Testament of Jesus Christ*, 3 Nephi 11:19-22, 12:1, 19:4

[100] *The Book of Mormon: Another Testament of Jesus Christ*, Moroni 4, 5

[101] *The Book of Mormon: Another Testament of Jesus Christ*, Moroni 11:27; *The Book of Mormon: Another Testament of Jesus Christ*, 2 Nephi 31:12, 18, 17, 7, 10, 13; 31:5, 13; *The Book of Mormon: Another Testament of Jesus Christ*, Mosiah 21:33, 18:10, 8-9, 13, 10, 15-16, 5:2, 27:25, *The Book of Mormon: Another Testament of Jesus Christ*, Alma 7:14-15, 4:4-5, 26:4, 23:5, 26:22, 13, 5:60; *The Book of Mormon: Another Testament of Jesus Christ*, Helaman 5:19, 3:26, 24, 16:5, 1, 4; *The Book of Mormon: Another Testament of Jesus Christ*, 3 Nephi 11:21-22, 25, 26:16, 30:2, 12:1-2, 1:23, 22:10, 7:25, 26:17, 28:18, 11:26, 7:24, 11:24-25, 34, 28:23, 27:20, 11:23; *The Book of Mormon: Another Testament of Jesus Christ*, 4 Nephi 1:1-2; *The Book of Mormon: Another Testament of Jesus Christ*, Mormon 7:7-8, 9:23, 29; *The Book of Mormon: Another Testament of Jesus Christ*, Ether 4:18; *The Book of Mormon: Another Testament of Jesus Christ*, Moroni 8:10-11, 15, 14, 19, 21, 9, 6:1-3, 8:25, 7:34

[102] *The Book of Mormon: Another Testament of Jesus Christ*, Mosiah 21:33; *The Book of Mormon: Another Testament of Jesus Christ*, 3 Nephi 11:21, 22, 25

[103] *The Book of Mormon: Another Testament of Jesus Christ*, 3 Nephi 11:23-28

[104] *The Book of Mormon: Another Testament of Jesus Christ*, 3 Nephi 11:21-28

[105] *The Book of Mormon: Another Testament of Jesus Christ*, Moroni 5:4-28

[106] *The Book of Mormon: Another Testament of Jesus Christ*, Moroni 8:19-21

[107] *The Book of Mormon: Another Testament of Jesus Christ*, Moroni 8:22

[108] *The Book of Mormon: Another Testament of Jesus Christ,* Moroni 8:22

[109] *The Book of Mormon: Another Testament of Jesus Christ,* Moroni 8:10

[110] *The Book of Mormon: Another Testament of Jesus Christ,* Jacob 1:17, 2:11

[111] *The Book of Mormon: Another Testament of Jesus Christ,* Jacob 2:12-22

[112] *The Book of Mormon: Another Testament of Jesus Christ,* Jacob 2:23-35

[113] *The Book of Mormon: Another Testament of Jesus Christ,* Jacob 1:18-19

[114] *The Book of Mormon: Another Testament of Jesus Christ,* Alma 5:3

[115] *The Book of Mormon: Another Testament of Jesus Christ,* Alma 5

[116] *The Book of Mormon: Another Testament of Jesus Christ,* Alma 7

[117] *The Book of Mormon: Another Testament of Jesus Christ,* Alma 8:4

[118] *The Book of Mormon: Another Testament of Jesus Christ,* Alma 8:9

[119] *The Book of Mormon: Another Testament of Jesus Christ,* Alma 13:2-3

[120] *The Book of Mormon: Another Testament of Jesus Christ,* 3 Nephi 11:21-22

[121] *The Book of Mormon: Another Testament of Jesus Christ,* 3 Nephi 12:1

[122] *The Book of Mormon: Another Testament of Jesus Christ,* Moroni 6:1-4

[123] *The Book of Mormon: Another Testament of Jesus Christ,* Jacob 2:27

[124] *The Torah,* Genesis 4:19, 16:2-4, 6, 9, 21:12, 29:16; *The Torah,* Exodus 21:10; *The Torah,* Numbers 12:1; *The Torah,* Deuteronomy 17:17, 21:13, 15, 25:5; *The Nevi'im,* Judges 8:30, 19:1; *The Nevi'im,* 1 Samuel 1:2, 25:42; *The Nevi'im,* 2 Samuel 3:3, 12:8; *The Nevi'im,* 1 Kings 11:1; *The Nevi'im,* Isaiah 4:1; *The Ketuvim,* 1 Chronicles 14:3; *The Ketuvim,* 2 Chronicles 11:21, 23, 13:21, 24:3

[125] *The New Testament of Jesus Christ (KJV),* Titus 1:6-7

[126] *The Book of Mormon: Another Testament of Jesus Christ,* Jacob 2:27-28

[127] *The Torah,* Deuteronomy 21:10-15

[128] *The Torah,* Jacob 2:30

[129] *The Torah,* Jacob 2:30

[130] *The Book of Mormon: Another Testament of Jesus Christ,* Moroni 8:8

[131] *The Book of Mormon: Another Testament of Jesus Christ,* Moroni 8:9

[132] *The Book of Mormon: Another Testament of Jesus Christ,* Moroni 8:15

[133] *The Book of Mormon: Another Testament of Jesus Christ,* Moroni 8:22

[134] *The Book of Mormon: Another Testament of Jesus Christ,* 2 Nephi 5:16

[135] *The Book of Mormon: Another Testament of Jesus Christ,* Mosiah 2:5, 9, 5:10-11

[136] *The Book of Mormon: Another Testament of Jesus Christ,* 3 Nephi 11:1

[137] *The Book of Mormon: Another Testament of Jesus Christ,* 3 Nephi 11:8-10

[138] *The Book of Mormon: Another Testament of Jesus Christ,* 3 Nephi 11:13-15

[139] *The Book of Mormon: Another Testament of Jesus Christ,* 3 Nephi 11:23-41

[140] *The Book of Mormon: Another Testament of Jesus Christ,* 3 Nephi 12, 13, 14

[141] *The Book of Mormon: Another Testament of Jesus Christ,* 3 Nephi 17:8-10

[142] *The Book of Mormon: Another Testament of Jesus Christ,* 3 Nephi 17:11-18

[143] *The Book of Mormon: Another Testament of Jesus Christ,* 3 Nephi 17:21-22

[144] *The Book of Mormon: Another Testament of Jesus Christ,* 3 Nephi 17:23-24

[145] *The Book of Mormon: Another Testament of Jesus Christ,* Alma 17-26

[146] *The Book of Mormon: Another Testament of Jesus Christ,* Alma 17:12-14, 26:23-26

[147] *The Book of Mormon: Another Testament of Jesus Christ,* Mosiah 28:5

[148] *The Book of Mormon: Another Testament of Jesus Christ,* Mosiah 28:5-6

[149] *The Book of Mormon: Another Testament of Jesus Christ,* Mosiah 28:7-8

[150] *The Book of Mormon: Another Testament of Jesus Christ,* Mosiah 28:5

[151] *The Book of Mormon: Another Testament of Jesus Christ,* Alma 19:22

[152] *The Book of Mormon: Another Testament of Jesus Christ*, Alma 19:22

[153] *The Book of Mormon: Another Testament of Jesus Christ*, Alma 26:4, 22

[154] *The Book of Mormon: Another Testament of Jesus Christ*, Alma 18:22-43, 22:4-19

[155] *The Book of Mormon: Another Testament of Jesus Christ*, Alma 18:40-42, 22:17-18

[156] *The Book of Mormon: Another Testament of Jesus Christ*, Alma 26:4, 22, 30:3

[157] *The Book of Mormon: Another Testament of Jesus Christ*, Alma 28:3

[158] *The Book of Mormon: Another Testament of Jesus Christ*, Alma 17:5

[159] *The Book of Mormon: Another Testament of Jesus Christ*, 1 Nephi 1:19, 10:4-7, 9, 11, 11:13, 24, 27, 31-34; 12:6, 11, 13:37, 40; 14:14, 15:13, 20, 17:41, 19:8-10, 20:2, 21:13, 16, 22:15, 20, 21, 26; *The Book of Mormon: Another Testament of Jesus Christ*, 2 Nephi 1:15, 2:4, 7-9, 26-28, 6:9, 7:6, 8:8, 9:5-7, 10, 12, 15, 21-22, 25-26, 41, 10:3, 5, 25, 11:3, 6-7, 12:12, 19-20, 16:3, 17:14, 18:14, 19:6, 13, 22:2, 23:7-9, 13, 15, 25:13, 19, 26, 29, 26:1, 3-4, 9, 24-25, 33, 30:10, 31:10, 13, 16, 19-20, 32:3, 33:10; *The Book of Mormon: Another Testament of Jesus Christ*, Jacob 1:7-8, 4:4, 15-16, 5:75, 6:3, 7:12; *The Book of Mormon: Another Testament of Jesus Christ*, Enos 1:6, 27; *The Book of Mormon: Another Testament of Jesus Christ*, Jarom 1:11; *The Book of Mormon: Another Testament of Jesus Christ*, Omni 1:25, 26; *The Book of Mormon: Another Testament of Jesus Christ*, Mosiah 3:5-11, 13, 15, 16, 5:2, 8, 7:33, 13:28, 33-35, 14:3-5, 7, 9, 11-12, 15:1-3, 5-9, 11, 13-14, 19, 21, 23, 16:2,4,6-9, 14-15, 18:10, 27:31; *The Book of Mormon: Another Testament of Jesus Christ*, Alma 5:33, 7:7, 9-13, 9:17, 26, 10:21, 11:39-40, 42, 12:15, 28, 13:26, 16:20, 19:13, 21:9, 22:10, 14-15, 18, 26:37, 27:27, 32:27, 33:11, 15, 19, 22, 34:2, 6-10, 14-15, 37:33, 37, 46-47, 38:9, 39:15, 40:3, 42:8, 15, 23, 45:16; *The Book of Mormon:*

Another Testament of Jesus Christ, Helaman 3:28, 5:9, 12, 6:5, 8:14-15, 18, 20, 22, 13:6, 14:2-5, 8, 12, 14, 16, 18, 20; *The Book of Mormon: Another Testament of Jesus Christ,* 3 Nephi 1:9, 14-15, 19, 5:24, 8:20, 10:9, 11:8, 15

[160] *The Book of Mormon: Another Testament of Jesus Christ,* 1 Nephi 1:19, 10:4-7, 9, 11, 11:13, 24, 27, 31-34; 12:6, 11, 13:37, 40; 14:14, 15:13, 20, 17:41, 19:8-10, 20:2, 21:13, 16, 22:15, 20, 21, 26; *The Book of Mormon: Another Testament of Jesus Christ,* 2 Nephi 1:15, 2:4, 7-9, 26-28, 6:9, 7:6, 8:8, 9:5-7, 10, 12, 15, 21-22, 25-26, 41, 10:3, 5, 25, 11:3, 6-7, 12:12, 19-20, 16:3, 17:14, 18:14, 19:6, 13, 22:2, 23:7-9, 13, 15, 25:13, 19, 26, 29, 26:1, 3-4, 9, 24-25, 33, 30:10, 31:10, 13, 16, 19-20, 32:3, 33:10; *The Book of Mormon: Another Testament of Jesus Christ,* Jacob 1:7-8, 4:4, 15-16, 5:75, 6:3, 7:12; *The Book of Mormon: Another Testament of Jesus Christ,* Enos 1:6, 27; *The Book of Mormon: Another Testament of Jesus Christ,* Jarom 1:11; *The Book of Mormon: Another Testament of Jesus Christ,* Omni 1:25, 26; *The Book of Mormon: Another Testament of Jesus Christ,* Mosiah 3:5-11, 13, 15, 16, 5:2, 8, 7:33, 13:28, 33-35, 14:3-5, 7, 9, 11-12, 15:1-3, 5-9, 11, 13-14, 19, 21, 23, 16:2,4,6-9, 14-15, 18:10, 27:31; *The Book of Mormon: Another Testament of Jesus Christ,* Alma 5:33, 7:7, 9-13, 9:17, 26, 10:21, 11:39-40, 42, 12:15, 28, 13:26, 16:20, 19:13, 21:9, 22:10, 14-15, 18, 26:37, 27:27, 32:27, 33:11, 15, 19, 22, 34:2, 6-10, 14-15, 37:33, 37, 46-47, 38:9, 39:15, 40:3, 42:8, 15, 23, 45:16; *The Book of Mormon: Another Testament of Jesus Christ,* Helaman 3:28, 5:9, 12, 6:5, 8:14-15, 18, 20, 22, 13:6, 14:2-5, 8, 12, 14, 16, 18, 20; *c,* 14-15, 19, 5:24, 8:20, 10:9, 11:8, 15

[161] *The Book of Mormon: Another Testament of Jesus Christ,* 1 Nephi 13:37, 22:15; *The Book of Mormon: Another Testament of Jesus Christ,* 2 Nephi 12:12, 19-20, 23:7-9, 13, 15, 26:4; 30:10; *The Book of Mormon: Another Testament of Jesus Christ,* 3 Nephi 25:1-3, 5; *The Book of Mormon: Another Testament of Jesus Christ,* Alma 37:37, 45:16; *The Book of Mormon: Another Testament of Jesus Christ,* Ether 4:19, *The Book of Mormon: Another Testament of Jesus Christ,* Jacob 5:75, 6:3; *The Book of Mormon: Another Testament of Jesus Christ,*

Moroni 7:48, *The Book of Mormon: Another Testament of Jesus Christ,* Mosiah 16:2

[162] *The Book of Mormon: Another Testament of Jesus Christ,* 2 Nephi 12:19

[163] *The Book of Mormon: Another Testament of Jesus Christ,* 2 Nephi 23:9

[164] *The Book of Mormon: Another Testament of Jesus Christ,* 2 Nephi 12:19

[165] *The Book of Mormon: Another Testament of Jesus Christ,* Alma 45:16

[166] *The Book of Mormon: Another Testament of Jesus Christ,* Mosiah 16:2

[167] *The Book of Mormon: Another Testament of Jesus Christ,* Ether 3:2; *The Book of Mormon: Another Testament of Jesus Christ,* 2 Nephi 32:8

[168] *The Book of Mormon: Another Testament of Jesus Christ,* 1 Nephi 1:12, 5:10, 17, 21, 15:23-24, 19:23; *The Book of Mormon: Another Testament of Jesus Christ,* 2 Nephi 4:15, 6:5, 11:8, 31:20, 33:4; *The Book of Mormon: Another Testament of Jesus Christ,* 3 Nephi 10:14, 20:11, 23:5; *The Book of Mormon: Another Testament of Jesus Christ,* Alma 4:19, 13:20, 14:1, 17:2-3, 5, 31:5, 63:12; *The Book of Mormon: Another Testament of Jesus Christ,* Ether 4:8, 11-12; *The Book of Mormon: Another Testament of Jesus Christ,* Helaman 15:7; *The Book of Mormon: Another Testament of Jesus Christ,* Jarom 1:12; *The Book of Mormon: Another Testament of Jesus Christ,* Mormon 8:23; *The Book of Mormon: Another Testament of Jesus Christ,* Mosiah 1:3-5, 7, 25:5, 27:35; *The Book of Mormon: Another Testament of Jesus Christ,* Omni 1:17

[169] *The Book of Mormon: Another Testament of Jesus Christ,* 1 Nephi 8:33, 19:23; *The Book of Mormon: Another Testament of Jesus Christ,* 2 Nephi 9:42, 28:8; *The Book of Mormon: Another Testament of Jesus Christ,* Mosiah 3:18-19, 4:11-12, 19, 21:13; *The Book of Mormon: Another Testament of Jesus Christ,* Alma 4:13, 5:13, 10:11, 13:13-14,

28, 17:11, 23:6, 26:3, 12, 18, 29:14, 32:6, 13-14, 19, 38, 37:33-34, 38:13-14, 42:30, 62:41, 49; *The Book of Mormon: Another Testament of Jesus Christ,* Helaman 3:35; *The Book of Mormon: Another Testament of Jesus Christ,* 3 Nephi 11:38, 12:2, 13:10; *The Book of Mormon: Another Testament of Jesus Christ,* Ether 12:27, 29, 37; *The Book of Mormon: Another Testament of Jesus Christ,* Moroni 7:45, 8:10, 26

[170] *The Book of Mormon: Another Testament of Jesus Christ,* Alma 27:27; *The Book of Mormon: Another Testament of Jesus Christ,* 2 Nephi 31:19; *The Book of Mormon: Another Testament of Jesus Christ,* Alma 32:27; *The Book of Mormon: Another Testament of Jesus Christ,* 1 Nephi 12:11; *The Book of Mormon: Another Testament of Jesus Christ,* Helaman 8:15; *The Book of Mormon: Another Testament of Jesus Christ,* Mosiah 4:3; *The Book of Mormon: Another Testament of Jesus Christ,* Alma 33:22, 37:33, 34:17; *The Book of Mormon: Another Testament of Jesus Christ,* Mosiah 24:15; *The Book of Mormon: Another Testament of Jesus Christ,* Helaman 3:28; *The Book of Mormon: Another Testament of Jesus Christ,* 1 Nephi 12:11

[171] *The Book of Mormon: Another Testament of Jesus Christ,* Mosiah 3:12; *The Book of Mormon: Another Testament of Jesus Christ,* Alma 34:15-17; *The Book of Mormon: Another Testament of Jesus Christ,* Moroni 10:26; *The Book of Mormon: Another Testament of Jesus Christ,* Alma 42:24; *The Book of Mormon: Another Testament of Jesus Christ,* Helaman 12:23; *The Book of Mormon: Another Testament of Jesus Christ,* 3 Nephi 11:38; *The Book of Mormon: Another Testament of Jesus Christ,* Alma 34:37; *The Book of Mormon: Another Testament of Jesus Christ,* 2 Nephi 2:7, 21, 9:16, 23-24, 46, 28:8; *The Book of Mormon: Another Testament of Jesus Christ,* Mosiah 4:8, 10, 15:26, 16:4-5, 12, 27:25; *The Book of Mormon: Another Testament of Jesus Christ,* Alma 1:4, 3:27, 5:13, 21, 25, 31, 51, 9:12, 11:34, 37, 41, 12:26, 21:6, 22:6, 37:25, 26, 42:3, 5, 13; *The Book of Mormon: Another Testament of Jesus Christ,* Helaman 14:18-19; *The Book of Mormon: Another Testament of Jesus Christ,* 3 Nephi 11:32, 12:19, 28:34; *The Book of Mormon: Another Testament of Jesus Christ,* Mormon 9:3-4;

The Book of Mormon: Another Testament of Jesus Christ, Moroni 7:34, 8:10, 19, 9:26

[172] *The Book of Mormon: Another Testament of Jesus Christ,* Moroni 11:27; *The Book of Mormon: Another Testament of Jesus Christ,* 2 Nephi 31:12, 18, 17, 7, 10, 13; 31:5, 13; *The Book of Mormon: Another Testament of Jesus Christ,* Mosiah 21:33, 18:10, 8-9, 13, 10, 15-16, 5:2, 27:25, *The Book of Mormon: Another Testament of Jesus Christ,* Alma 7:14-15, 4:4-5, 26:4, 23:5, 26:22, 13, 5:60; *The Book of Mormon: Another Testament of Jesus Christ,* Helaman 5:19, 3:26, 24, 16:5, 1, 4; *The Book of Mormon: Another Testament of Jesus Christ,* 3 Nephi 11:21-22, 25, 26:16, 30:2, 12:1-2, 1:23, 22:10, 7:25, 26:17, 28:18, 11:26, 7:24, 11:24-25, 34, 28:23, 27:20, 11:23; *The Book of Mormon: Another Testament of Jesus Christ,* 4 Nephi 1:1-2; *The Book of Mormon: Another Testament of Jesus Christ,* Mormon 7:7-8, 9:23, 29; *The Book of Mormon: Another Testament of Jesus Christ,* Ether 4:18; *The Book of Mormon: Another Testament of Jesus Christ,* Moroni 8:10-11, 15, 14, 19, 21, 9, 6:1-3, 8:25, 7:34

[173] *The Book of Mormon: Another Testament of Jesus Christ,* 2 Nephi 32:5; *The Book of Mormon: Another Testament of Jesus Christ,* Moroni 6:9; *The Book of Mormon: Another Testament of Jesus Christ,* 1 Nephi 4:6; *The Book of Mormon: Another Testament of Jesus Christ,* Alma 21:16; *The Book of Mormon: Another Testament of Jesus Christ,* Mosiah 3:19

[174] *The Book of Mormon: Another Testament of Jesus Christ,* Jacob 2:27, 34-35; 3 Nephi 12:27-30

[175] *The Book of Mormon: Another Testament of Jesus Christ,* Jacob 2:27, 34-35

[176] *The Book of Mormon: Another Testament of Jesus Christ,* Mosiah 13:12-24

[177] *The Book of Mormon: Another Testament of Jesus Christ,* 1 Nephi 12:9; *The Book of Mormon: Another Testament of Jesus Christ,* 3 Nephi 14:1-3, 5; *The Book of Mormon: Another Testament of Jesus Christ,* Mosiah 4:17-18

[178] *The Book of Mormon: Another Testament of Jesus Christ,* Mosiah 4:16-27; *The Book of Mormon: Another Testament of Jesus Christ,* Moroni 7:44-48

[179] *The Book of Mormon: Another Testament of Jesus Christ,* Mosiah 2:17, 21

[180] *The Book of Mormon: Another Testament of Jesus Christ,* Moroni 7:40-44

[181] *The Book of Mormon: Another Testament of Jesus Christ,* 1 Nephi 1:18-20; *The Book of Mormon: Another Testament of Jesus Christ,* 2 Nephi 1:4

[182] *The Book of Mormon: Another Testament of Jesus Christ,* 1 Nephi 2:7, 5:9, 7:22; *The Book of Mormon: Another Testament of Jesus Christ,* 2 Nephi 25:24, 30, 26:29; *The Book of Mormon: Another Testament of Jesus Christ,* Jacob 4:5; *The Book of Mormon: Another Testament of Jesus Christ,* Jarom 1:11; *The Book of Mormon: Another Testament of Jesus Christ,* Omni 1:26; *The Book of Mormon: Another Testament of Jesus Christ,* Mosiah 2:3-4, 3:15, 13:27-28, 30-32, 16:14; *The Book of Mormon: Another Testament of Jesus Christ,* Alma 15:16, 24:23, 25:15, 26:30, 34:10, 13-14, 38:12, 39:9; *The Book of Mormon: Another Testament of Jesus Christ,* Helaman 8:25, 10:4; *The Book of Mormon: Another Testament of Jesus Christ,* 3 Nephi 1:24, 9:17, 19-20, 11:11, 12:17-18, 30, 46, 13:19, 15:4-5; *The Book of Mormon: Another Testament of Jesus Christ,* 4 Nephi 1:12; *The Book of Mormon: Another Testament of Jesus Christ,* Mormon 2:14, 4:14, 21; *The Book of Mormon: Another Testament of Jesus Christ,* Ether 12:11

[183] *The Book of Mormon: Another Testament of Jesus Christ,* 3 Nephi 15:2-10

[184] *The Book of Mormon: Another Testament of Jesus Christ,* Alma 34:13-14, 25:15; *The Book of Mormon: Another Testament of Jesus Christ,* Mosiah 3:15, 13:27, 31, 16:14; *The Book of Mormon: Another Testament of Jesus Christ,* 2 Nephi 25:24; *The Book of Mormon: Another Testament of Jesus Christ,* Jacob 4:5; *The Book of Mormon: Another Testament of Jesus Christ,* 3 Nephi 9:19

[185] *The Book of Mormon: Another Testament of Jesus Christ*, 1 Nephi 11:33; *The Book of Mormon: Another Testament of Jesus Christ*, 2 Nephi 9:7; *The Book of Mormon: Another Testament of Jesus Christ*, Mosiah 14:11, 15:9, 16:15; *The Book of Mormon: Another Testament of Jesus Christ*, Alma 7:12, 22:14, 34:8, 10, 14, 39:15, 42:15; *The Book of Mormon: Another Testament of Jesus Christ*, 1 Nephi 12:11; *The Book of Mormon: Another Testament of Jesus Christ*, 2 Nephi 9:21, 25-26; *The Book of Mormon: Another Testament of Jesus Christ*, Mosiah 3:7, 11, 14:5, 14:12, 15:8-9; *The Book of Mormon: Another Testament of Jesus Christ*, Alma 5:33, 7:11-13, 12:15; 33:22, 34:8, 10, 14-15, 42:15, 23; *The Book of Mormon: Another Testament of Jesus Christ*, Helaman 14:18; *The Book of Mormon: Another Testament of Jesus Christ*, 3 Nephi 11:11, 14; *The Book of Mormon: Another Testament of Jesus Christ*, Moroni 8:19, 9:25

[186] *The Book of Mormon: Another Testament of Jesus Christ*, Mosiah 3:12; *The Book of Mormon: Another Testament of Jesus Christ*, Alma 34:16; *The Book of Mormon: Another Testament of Jesus Christ*, Moroni 10:26; *The Book of Mormon: Another Testament of Jesus Christ*, Alma 42:24; *The Book of Mormon: Another Testament of Jesus Christ*, Helaman 12:23; *The Book of Mormon: Another Testament of Jesus Christ*, 3 Nephi 11:38; *The Book of Mormon: Another Testament of Jesus Christ*, Alma 34:37; *The Book of Mormon: Another Testament of Jesus Christ*, 2 Nephi 2:7, 21, 9:16, 23-24, 46, 28:8; *The Book of Mormon: Another Testament of Jesus Christ*, Mosiah 4:8, 10, 15:26, 16:4-5, 12, 27:25; *The Book of Mormon: Another Testament of Jesus Christ*, Alma 1:4, 3:27, 5:13, 21, 25, 31, 51, 9:12, 11:34, 37, 41, 12:26, 21:6, 22:6, 37:25, 26, 42:3, 5, 13; *The Book of Mormon: Another Testament of Jesus Christ*, Helaman 14:18-19; *The Book of Mormon: Another Testament of Jesus Christ*, 3 Nephi 11:32, 12:19, 28:34; *The Book of Mormon: Another Testament of Jesus Christ*, Mormon 9:3-4; *The Book of Mormon: Another Testament of Jesus Christ*, Moroni 7:34, 8:10, 19, 9:26; *The Book of Mormon: Another Testament of Jesus Christ*, Alma 34:15-17

[187] *The Book of Mormon: Another Testament of Jesus Christ*, 3 Nephi 15:2-10

Endnotes—Chapter 4, The New Testament of Jesus Christ

[1] 50 Torah, Nevi'im, and Ketuvim prophecies of the Messiah, and their New Testament fulfillment:

(#) Prophecy Fulfillment	Book	Chapter	Verse
(1) a virgin shall conceive	Isaiah	7	14
virgin shall be with child…bring forth a son…call his name Emmanuel…interpreted…God with us	Matthew	1	23
(2) thou, Bethlehem..though thou be little…out of thee shall he come forth…ruler in Israel	Micah	5	2
thou Bethlehem…art not the least among the princes of Juda…come a Governor…rule	Matthew	2	6
(3) in Ramah, lamentation, and bitter weeping; Rachel weeping for her children…they were not	Jeremiah	31	15
Herod...slew all the children that were in Bethlahem	Matthew	2	16
(4) I loved him, and called my son out of Egypt	Hosea	11	1
was there until the death of Herod…fulfilled which was spoken…Out of Egypt…called my son	Matthew	2	15
(5) come a Star out of Jacob	Numbers	24	17
Jesus Christ	Matthew	1	1
Abraham begat Isaac…begat Jacob…Judah…Phares	Matthew	1	2
(6) righteous Branch	Jeremiah	23	5
Jesus Christ	Matthew	1	1
(7) stem of Jesse	Isaiah	11	1

Jesus Christ	Matthew	1	1
Salmon begat Booz of Rachab…Booz begat Obed of Ruth…Obed begat Jesse	Matthew	1	5
And Jesse begat David the king; and David the king begat Solomon	Matthew	1	6
(8) The Lord thy God will raise up unto thee a Prophet from the midst…hearken	Deuteronomy	18	15
Prophet…like unto thee	Deuteronomy	18	18
The woman saith unto him, Sir, I perceive that thou art a prophet	John	4	19
(9) his name shall be called…Prince of Peace	Isaiah	9	6
let not your heart be troubled, neither let it be afraid	John	14	27
(10) voice of him…crieth in the wilderness, Prepare ye the way of the Lord, make straight	Isaiah	40	3
one crying in the wilderness, Prepare ye the way of the Lord, make his paths straight	Luke	3	4
writen in the prophets…I send my messenger…prepare thy way before thee	Mark	1	2
voice of one crying in the wilderness, Prepare ye the way of the Lord…paths straight	Mark	1	3
(11) To open the blind eyes, to bring out the prisoners from the prison	Isaiah	42	7
Behold my servant…beloved…put my spirit upon him…he shall shew judgment…Gentiles	Matthew	12	18
(12) I will open my mouth in a parable	Psalm	78	2
Watch ye therefore: for ye know not when the master of the house cometh	Mark	13	35

(13) neither was any deceit in his mouth	Isaiah	53	9
I am the way…truth…life: no man cometh unto the Father, but by me	John	14	6
(14) land of Zebulun…land of Naphtali…people walked in darkness have seen a great light	Isaiah	9	1
he came and dwelt in Capernaum…in the borders of Zabulon and Nephthalim	Matthew	4	13
might be fulfilled…Esaias…land of Zabulon…Nephthalim…people…saw great light	Matthew	4	14
The land of Zabulon, and the land of Nephtalim, by the way of the sea	Matthew	4	15
(15) walked in darkness…see a…light	Isaiah	9	2
The people which sat in darkness saw great light	Matthew	4	16
(16) Hear ye indeed, but understand not…see ye indeed, but perceive not	Isaiah	6	9
prophecy of Esaias…hearing ye shall hear…not understand…seeing…see...not perceive	Matthew	13	14
(17) he hath sent me to bind up the brokenhearted, to proclaim liberty to the captives	Isaiah	61	1
Neither do I condemn thee: go, and sin no more	John	8	11
(18) behold, thy King cometh unto thee	Zechariah	9	9
hosanna: Blessed is the King of Israel	John	12	13
Behold, thy King cometh unto thee, meek, and sitting upon an ass, and a colt	Matthew	21	5
they that followed, cried, saying, Hosanna; Blessed is he that cometh in the name…Lord	Mark	11	9

Blessed be the kingdom of our father David, that cometh in the name of the Lord: Hosanna	Mark	11	10
(19) riding upon an ass, and upon a colt	Zechariah	9	9
Jesus, when he had found a young ass, sat thereon	John	12	14
ass…colt…hosanna	Matthew	21	7
ye shall find a colt tied, whereon never man sat; loose him, and bring him	Mark	11	2
(20) precious corner stone	Isaiah	28	16
The stone which the builders rejected…same is become the head of the corner	Matthew	21	42
(21) stone…builders refused	Psalm	118	22
The stone which the builders rejected…same is become the head of the corner	Matthew	21	42
This is the stone which was set at nought of you builders…become…head…corner	Acts	4	11
(22) waves…thou stillest them	Psalm	89	9
peace, be still…wind ceased, and there was a great calm	Mark	4	39
(23) he maketh the storm a calm	Psalm	107	29
peace, be still…wind ceased, and there was a great calm	Mark	4	39
(24) Saviour…he bare them, and carried them all the days of old	Isaiah	63	9
his sweat was as it were great drops of blood falling down to the ground	Luke	22	44
(25) pleased the Lord to bruise him	Isaiah	53	10
shewed by…prophets…Christ should suffer, he hath so fulfilled	Acts	3	18
(26) for the transgression of my people was he stricken	Isaiah	53	8

his sweat was as it were great drops of blood falling down to the ground	Luke	22	44
(27) he was wounded for our transgressions	Isaiah	53	5
his sweat was as it were great drops of blood falling down to the ground	Luke	22	44
(28) Surely he hath borne our griefs, and carried our sorrow	Isaiah	53	4
Esaias…Himself took our infirmities, and bare our sicknesses	Matthew	8	17
(29) mine…friend…lifted up his heel	Psalm	41	9
Then one of the twelve, called Judas Iscariot, went unto the chief priests	Matthew	26	14
(30) sold the righteous for silver	Amos	2	6
thirty pieces of silver	Matthew	26	15
(31) So they weighed for my price thirty pieces of silver	Zechariah	11	12
(31) And I took the thirty pieces of silver, and cast them to the potter in the house of the Lord	Zechariah	11	13
fulfilled…Jeremy the prophet…they took the thirty pieces of silver, the price	Matthew	27	9
(32) They that hate me without a cause	Psalm	69	6
fulfilled that is written in their law, They hated me without a cause	John	15	25
(33) I was like a lamb or an ox that is brought to the slaughter	Jeremiah	11	19
Caiaphas	Matthew	26	57
(34) smite the shepherd, and the sheep shall be scattered	Zechariah	13	7
Then all the disciples forsook him	Matthew	26	56
And they all forsook him, and fled	Mark	14	50

be offended because of me this night..I will smite the shepherd…sheep…scattered	Matthew	14	27
be offended because of me this night…written…smite the shepherd…scattered	Matthew	26	31
(35) gave my back to the smiters	Isaiah	50	6
released he Barabbas unto them…scourged Jesus…delivered him to be crucified	Matthew	27	26
Pilate, willing to content the people, released Barabbas…Jesus..scourged him…crucified	Mark	15	15
Pilate therefore took Jesus, and scourged him	John	19	1
(36) he giveth his cheek	Lamentations	3	30
they spit in his face, and buffeted him…others smote him with the palms…hands	Matthew	26	67
(37) smiteth him	Lamentations	3	30
they spit in his face, and buffeted him…others smote him with the palms…hands	Matthew	26	67
(38) nail in his holy place	Ezra	9	8
(38) nail in a sure place	Isaiah	22	23
(38) out of him came forth…the nail	Zechariah	10	4
I shall see in his hands the print of the nails, and put my finger into the print of the nails	John	20	25
(39) they pierced my hands	Psalm	22	16
I shall see in his hands the print of the nails, and put my finger into the print of the nails	John	20	25

(40) he was numbered with the transgressors	Isaiah	53	12
scripture was fulfilled…he was numbered with the transgressors	Mark	15	28
(41) He trusted on the Lord that he would deliver him: let him deliver him	Psalm	22	8
Save thyself, and come down from the cross	Mark	15	30
Likewise also the chief priests mocking said…with the scribes…saved others; himself	Mark	15	31
(42) wag his head	Jeremiah	18	16
they that passed by railed on him, wagging their heads	Mark	15	29
Save thyself, and come down from the cross	Mark	15	30
(43) They gave me also gall for my meat; and in my thirst they gave me vinegar to drink	Psalm	69	21
one ran and filled a spunge full of vinegar, and put it on a reed, and gave him to drink	Mark	15	34
(44) my God, my God, why hast thou forsaken	Psalm	22	1
Jesus cried with a loud voice…"My God, my God, why hast thou forsaken me?"	Mark	15	36
(45) into thine hand I commit my spirit	Psalm	31	5
Father, into thy hands I commend my spirit	Luke	23	46
(46) they shall look upon me whom they have pierced	Zechariah	12	10
They shall look on him whom they pierced	John	19	37
(47) He keepeth all his bones: not one of them is broken	Psalm	69	21

scripture should be fulfilled, A bone of him shall not be broken	John	19	36
(48) They part my garments among them, and cast lots upon my vesture	Psalm	22	18
they parted his raiment, and cast lots	Luke	23	34
fulfilled…parted my garments among them…upon my vesture did they cast lots	Matthew	27	35
they had crucified him, they parted his garments, casting lots upon them	Mark	15	24
scripture might be fulfilled…They parted my raiment among them…my vesture…cast lots	John	19	24
(49) he made his grave with the wicked…neither was any deceit in his mouth	Isaiah	53	9
with him they crucify two thieves; the one on his right hand, and the other on his left	Mark	15	27
(50) Messiah be cut off	Daniel	9	26
Father, into thy hands I commend my spirit	Luke	23	46

[2] *The New Testament of Jesus Christ (KJV)*, Matthew 17:5, 22:44, 26:63; *The New Testament of Jesus Christ (KJV)*, Mark 9:7, 12:36; *The New Testament of Jesus Christ (KJV)*, Luke 1:35, 3:22; *The New Testament of Jesus Christ (KJV)*, John 1:14, 34, 6:69, 9:37, 10:36, 11:27; *The New Testament of Jesus Christ (KJV)*, Romans 1:4; *The New Testament of Jesus Christ (KJV)*, Colossians 1:15; *The New Testament of Jesus Christ (KJV)*, Hebrews 1:5

[3] *The New Testament of Jesus Christ (KJV)*, John 17:23-25, 16:5, 16, 17:13, 8:42, 12:49, 14:24, 15:21, 17:8, 18, 3:16, 8:29, 3:35, 5:20; *The New Testament of Jesus Christ (KJV)*, 1 Peter 1:20; *The New Testament of Jesus Christ (KJV)*, John 8:58, 5:19

[4] *The New Testament of Jesus Christ (KJV)*, Matthew 5-7

[5] *The New Testament of Jesus Christ (KJV)*, Acts 1:24-26, 22; *The New Testament of Jesus Christ (KJV)*, Matthew 4:20-21, 9:9, 10:1; *The New Testament of Jesus Christ (KJV)*, Mark 2:14, 1:17, 6:7; *The New Testament of Jesus Christ (KJV)*, John 15:16; *The New Testament of Jesus Christ (KJV)*, Luke 6:13; *The New Testament of Jesus Christ (KJV)*, Ephesians 2:20, 4:11, 1:22; *The New Testament of Jesus Christ (KJV)*, Colossians 1:18

[6] *The New Testament of Jesus Christ (KJV)*, 1 John 1:9, 7; *The New Testament of Jesus Christ (KJV)*, Revelation 12:11, 1:5; *The New Testament of Jesus Christ (KJV)*, 1 Timothy 2:6; *The New Testament of Jesus Christ (KJV)*, Matthew 9:6, 1:21, 26:38, 36, 40, 37, 39, 42; *The New Testament of Jesus Christ (KJV)*, Acts 5:31, 10:43, 12; *The New Testament of Jesus Christ (KJV)*, Hebrews 10:12; *The New Testament of Jesus Christ (KJV)*, Luke 4:18, 24:46, 22:43-44; *The New Testament of Jesus Christ (KJV)*, Philippians 4:13; *The New Testament of Jesus Christ (KJV)*, Mark 2:10, 14:32-34; *The New Testament of Jesus Christ (KJV)*, John 18:11, 19:17; *The New Testament of Jesus Christ (KJV)*, 1 Corinthians 15:3

[7] *The New Testament of Jesus Christ (KJV)*, Luke 11:28; *The New Testament of Jesus Christ (KJV)*, Matthew 7:24, 19:21; *The New Testament of Jesus Christ (KJV)*, John 14:15, 21:22, 13:15; *The New Testament of Jesus Christ (KJV)*, Colossians 2:6; *The New Testament of Jesus Christ (KJV)*, Revelation 14:4; *The New Testament of Jesus Christ (KJV)*, Galatians 3:27

[8] *The New Testament of Jesus Christ (KJV)*, Matthew 4:17; *The New Testament of Jesus Christ (KJV)*, Luke 4:17

[9] *The New Testament of Jesus Christ (KJV)*, Matthew 11:28, 19:21; *The New Testament of Jesus Christ (KJV)*, Luke 9:60, 18:22; *The New Testament of Jesus Christ (KJV)*, Revelation 22:17

[10] *The New Testament of Jesus Christ (KJV)*, Matthew 26-27; *The New Testament of Jesus Christ (KJV)*, Mark 14-15; *The New Testament of Jesus Christ (KJV)*, Luke 23:6; *The New Testament of Jesus Christ (KJV)*, John 16:32, 18-19

[11] *The New Testament of Jesus Christ (KJV)*, Matthew 26:62-63; *The New Testament of Jesus Christ (KJV)*, Acts 8:32

[12] *The New Testament of Jesus Christ (KJV)*, Matthew 27:29-56; *The New Testament of Jesus Christ (KJV)*, Mark 15; *The New Testament of Jesus Christ (KJV)*, Luke 23:33-34; *The New Testament of Jesus Christ (KJV)*, John 10:18, *The New Testament of Jesus Christ (KJV)*, 19:6, 17-34; *The New Testament of Jesus Christ (KJV)*, Acts 3:15

[13] *The New Testament of Jesus Christ (KJV)*, Luke 24:2-6; *The New Testament of Jesus Christ (KJV)*, John 20:1-6

[14] *The New Testament of Jesus Christ (KJV)*, John 20:2, 11-13, 15-16; *The New Testament of Jesus Christ (KJV)*, Mark 16:8-9

[15] *The New Testament of Jesus Christ (KJV)*, Matthew 28:9-10; *The New Testament of Jesus Christ (KJV)*, Mark 16:14; *The New Testament of Jesus Christ (KJV)*, 1 Corinthians 15:6; *The New Testament of Jesus Christ (KJV)*, Acts 2:32, *The New Testament of Jesus Christ (KJV)*, 13:31; *The New Testament of Jesus Christ (KJV)*, Luke 24:39

[16] *The New Testament of Jesus Christ (KJV)*, Acts 1:11

[17] *The New Testament of Jesus Christ (KJV)*, Matthew 26:39; *The New Testament of Jesus Christ (KJV)*, John 12:27-28

[18] *The New Testament of Jesus Christ (KJV)*, Mark 1:35, 6:46, 14:35-36; *The New Testament of Jesus Christ (KJV)*, John 17, 11:41-42, 12:27-28; *The New Testament of Jesus Christ (KJV)*, Matthew 19:13, 26:36-44; *The New Testament of Jesus Christ (KJV)*, Luke 3:21, 6:12, 9:28, 22:31-32

[19] *The New Testament of Jesus Christ (KJV)*, John 11:41-42

[20] *The New Testament of Jesus Christ (KJV)*, Matthew 26:36-44

[21] *The New Testament of Jesus Christ (KJV)*, Mark 14:35-36

[22] *The New Testament of Jesus Christ (KJV)*, Luke 23:34

[23] *The New Testament of Jesus Christ (KJV)*, Luke 23:36

[24] *The New Testament of Jesus Christ (KJV)*, Luke 23:46

[25] *The New Testament of Jesus Christ (KJV)*, Mark 15:37

[26] *The New Testament of Jesus Christ (KJV)*, Luke 3:22; *The New Testament of Jesus Christ (KJV)*, Mark 9:7; *The New Testament of*

Jesus Christ (KJV), Matthew 17:5; *The New Testament of Jesus Christ (KJV),* Romans 1:4

[27] *The New Testament of Jesus Christ (KJV),* John 1:14

[28] *The New Testament of Jesus Christ (KJV),* Colossians 1:15

[29] *The New Testament of Jesus Christ (KJV),* Acts 17:29

[30] *The New Testament of Jesus Christ (KJV),* John 1:14

[31] *The New Testament of Jesus Christ (KJV),* Matthew 1:18; *The New Testament of Jesus Christ (KJV),* Luke 2:8, 11, 16, 21

[32] *The New Testament of Jesus Christ (KJV),* Luke 1:35

[33] *The New Testament of Jesus Christ (KJV),* Luke 1:34

[34] *The New Testament of Jesus Christ (KJV),* Matthew 1:20

[35] *The New Testament of Jesus Christ (KJV),* Matthew 1:24

[36] *The New Testament of Jesus Christ (KJV),* Matthew 1:25

[37] *The Nevi'im,* Isaiah 7:14

[38] *The Ketuvim,* Psalm 96:13; *The Nevi'im,* Isaiah 2:19; *The Nevi'im,* Ezekiel 43:2; *The Nevi'im,* Isaiah 10:17, 24:6, 66:15; *The Nevi'im,* Malachi 3:2, 4:1; *The Ketuvim,* Psalm 9:8; *The Ketuvim,* Psalm 96:13; *The Nevi'im,* Isaiah 2:12; *The Nevi'im,* Isaiah 10:17, 13:6, 9, 13, 19, 24:1, 6, 26:5, 66:15; *The Nevi'im,* Joel 1:15, 2:11; *The Nevi'im,* Malachi 3:2, 4:1; *The Nevi'im,* Isaiah 26:5; *The Nevi'im,* Zechariah 14:4-5

[39] *The New Testament of Jesus Christ (KJV),* Matthew 4:17

[40] *The New Testament of Jesus Christ (KJV),* Matthew 11:28-30; *The New Testament of Jesus Christ (KJV),* Mark 5:36

[41] *The New Testament of Jesus Christ (KJV),* Matthew 4:17, 12:41, 11:20-21; *The New Testament of Jesus Christ (KJV),* Luke 3:3, 9, 5:32

[42] *The New Testament of Jesus Christ (KJV), The New Testament of Jesus Christ (KJV),* John 3-5, *The New Testament of Jesus Christ (KJV),* Matthew 3:15; *The New Testament of Jesus Christ (KJV),* Mark 16:16

[43] *The New Testament of Jesus Christ (KJV),* Matthew 3:13-17

[44] *The New Testament of Jesus Christ (KJV),* Matthew 5:3

[45] *The New Testament of Jesus Christ (KJV),* Matthew 5:4
[46] *The New Testament of Jesus Christ (KJV),* Matthew 5:5
[47] *The New Testament of Jesus Christ (KJV),* Matthew 5:6
[48] *The New Testament of Jesus Christ (KJV),* Matthew 5:7
[49] *The New Testament of Jesus Christ (KJV),* Matthew 5:8
[50] *The New Testament of Jesus Christ (KJV),* Matthew 5:9
[51] *The New Testament of Jesus Christ (KJV),* Matthew 5:10
[52] *The New Testament of Jesus Christ (KJV),* Matthew 5:11
[53] *The New Testament of Jesus Christ (KJV),* Matthew 5:14
[54] *The New Testament of Jesus Christ (KJV),* Matthew 5:16
[55] *The New Testament of Jesus Christ (KJV),* Matthew 5:21
[56] *The New Testament of Jesus Christ (KJV),* Matthew 5:22
[57] *The New Testament of Jesus Christ (KJV),* Matthew 5:27
[58] *The New Testament of Jesus Christ (KJV),* Matthew 5:28
[59] *The New Testament of Jesus Christ (KJV),* Matthew 5:31
[60] *The New Testament of Jesus Christ (KJV),* Matthew 5:32
[61] *The New Testament of Jesus Christ (KJV),* Matthew 5:33
[62] *The New Testament of Jesus Christ (KJV),* Matthew 5:34
[63] *The New Testament of Jesus Christ (KJV),* Matthew 5:37
[64] *The New Testament of Jesus Christ (KJV),* Matthew 5:38
[65] *The New Testament of Jesus Christ (KJV),* Matthew 5:39
[66] *The New Testament of Jesus Christ (KJV),* Matthew 5:40
[67] *The New Testament of Jesus Christ (KJV),* Matthew 5:44-47
[68] *The New Testament of Jesus Christ (KJV),* Matthew 5:48
[69] *The New Testament of Jesus Christ (KJV),* Matthew 6:5-14
[70] *The New Testament of Jesus Christ (KJV),* Matthew 7:1
[71] *The New Testament of Jesus Christ (KJV),* Matthew 7:2

Endnotes—Chapter 5, The Holy Qur'an

[1] *The Holy Qur'an* 33:21; 11:31. 2:104, 3:153, 3:144

[2] *The Holy Qur'an* 2:22, 54, 143, 160, 163, 173, 182, 192, 199, 218, 226, 3:31, 74, 89, 129, 132, 4:16-17, 23, 25, 27, 64, 96, 100, 106, 129, 152, 5:34, 39, 51, 74, 97, 6:54, 133, 147, 155, 157, 165, 7:56, 151, 153, 156, 167, 8:69-70, 9:5, 15, 27, 99, 102, 104, 117, 118, 128, 10:107, 11:41, 90, 12:53, 92, 98, 14:36, 15:49, 16:7, 18, 47, 115 119, 17:54, 66, 18:58, 22:60, 65, 118, 24:5, 22, 15:6, 70, 26:9, 68, 104, 122, 140, 159, 175, 191, 217, 28:16, 30:5, 32:6, 33:5, 24, 43, 50, 59, 73, 34:2, 36:5, 56, 39:53, 40:3, 41:32, 42:5, 8, 44:42, 45:30, 46:8, 48:14, 49:5, 12, 14, 52:28, 55:1, 57:9, 57:21, 28, 29, 58:12, 59:22, 60:1, 7, 8-9, 12, 62:11, 66:1, 67:19, 73:20

[3] *The Holy Qur'an* 8:51, 26:209, 3:108, 4:135, 5:8, 7:29, 16:90, 18:49, 22:9, 28:70, 28:88, 40:31, 41:46, 45:10, 50:29, 75:14

[4] *The Holy Qur'an* 2:20, 106, 109, 148, 228, 241, 260, 184, 286, 3:26, 29, 126, 189, 4:149, 165, 5:17, 40, 120, 6:16, 7:42, 8:41, 49, 52, 9:39-40, 71, 10:73, 11:4, 13:13, 16, 41, 14:4, 48, 16:40, 59, 70, 77, 18:45, 22:6, 40, 74, 24:45, 26:9, 68, 104, 122, 140, 159, 175, 191, 217, 27:9, 78, 29:20, 26, 42, 30:6, 27, 50, 54, 31:9, 27, 32:6, 33:17, 25, 27, 34:27, 35:1-2, 28, 44, 36:5, 83, 38:9, 65-66, 39:1, 4-5, 37, 44, 62, 40:2, 8, 16, 41:12, 39, 42:3-4, 9, 19, 49, 42:50, 44:42, 45:2, 37, 46:2, 33, 48:4, 6, 19, 21, 54:42, 54, 56:74, 96, 57:1-2, 25, 58:2, 59:1, 6, 23, 24, 60:7, 61:1, 62:3, 64:1, 18, 67:1-2

[5] *The Holy Qur'an* 2:29-30, 32-33, 74, 77, 85, 96, 110, 115, 137, 140, 144, 181, 224, 231, 235, 244, 256, 261, 265, 268, 282, 3:29, 34, 73, 119, 154, 156, 180, 4:11-12, 17, 24, 32, 92, 111, 126, 148, 170, 176, 5:7-8, 51, 76, 97, 109, 116, 6:3, 13, 18, 59, 73, 83, 103, 115, 128, 139, 7:200, 8:17, 42, 43, 53, 62, 71, 74, 75, 9:15, 28, 60, 78, 97-98, 103, 106, 110, 115, 10:20, 61, 65, 11:5, 31, 111-112, 123, 12:6, 34, 76, 83, 100, 13:9, 42, 14:38, 15:25, 86, 16:19, 23, 70, 91, 17:54, 21:4, 81, 22:52, 59, 24:18, 21, 32, 35, 58, 60, 64, 25:58, 26:220, 27:6, 78, 87, 93, 29:5, 10, 45, 52, 30:54, 60, 62, 31:23, 29, 34, 32:6, 33:1, 9, 40, 50, 51, 34:48, 35:11, 31, 44, 36:76, 81, 39:70, 40:2, 20, 56, 41:12, 36, 40, 42:24-25, 50, 43:84, 44:6, 47:26, 30, 48:4, 11, 48:26, 49:1, 8, 13, 16,

18, 51:30, 57:3-5, 10, 58:3, 7, 11, 59:18, 22, 60:1-2, 10, 64:2, 4, 8, 11, 18, 66:2, 67:13-14, 19,76:30

[6] *The Holy Qur'an* 2:34, 6:98, 7:11, 15:34, 17:61, 18:50, 19:67, 38:69, 73

[7] *The Holy Qur'an* 3:179, 4:136, 48:9, 64:8, 14:23, 5:93, 69, 2:62

[8] *The Holy Qur'an* 48:9, 4:136, 64:8, 47:2

[9] *The Holy Qur'an* 3:32, 132, 4:13, 59, 24:54, 47:33, 64, 12, 72:23, 4:69, 49:14

[10] *The Holy Qur'an* 2:61, 118, 209, 211, 213, 248, 253, 3:11, 19, 21, 41, 49, 103, 118, 183-184, 4:59, 155, 5:10, 86, 6:37, 39, 48, 97, 109, 126, 157-158, 7:40, 72, 146, 177, 8:29, 10:6, 13, 24, 35, 44, 101, 13:38, 14:5, 16:104, 17:97, 22:51, 25:62, 26:4, 7, 67, 103, 121, 139, 158, 174, 190, 27:52, 86, 29:15, 24, 35, 44, 50, 30:16-17, 20-21, 22-25, 37, 46, 31:31-21, 32:26, 34:9, 19, 36:37, 41, 46, 37:14, 39:42, 52, 40:4, 13, 63, 69, 41:37, 39, 53, 42:29, 32, 43:63, 45:3-5, 45:12-13, 46:27, 51:41, 43, 44, 54:15, 42, 64:10, 78:28

[11] *The Holy Qur'an* 4:162, 5:91, 6:72, 10:87, 11:114, 13:22, 17:78-79, 20:130, 22:35, 29:45, 30:31, 31:17, 73:2-3, 73:20, 76:25-26, 98:5, 40:60, 2:255, 10:3, 2:186, 14:39, 39:8, 39:49, 40:50, 2:43, 45, 83, 110, 144, 149, 153, 177, 238, 239, 277, 3:43, 61, 4:43, 77, 103, 162, 5:4, 6, 7:29, 55-56, 170, 180, 9:84, 10:88, 13:36, 14:31, 41, 16:53, 17:67, 110, 20:7, 130, 22:77-78, 23:27, 24:56, 26:213, 29:45, 30:31, 32:16, 53:62, 62:9, 70:34, 73:2-3, 96:19, 107:4, 108:8

[12] *The Holy Qur'an* 2:43, 83, 110, 177, 4:8, 77, 103, 162, 14:31, 17:26, 29, 21:35, 22:36, 78, 24:56, 30:39, 36:47, 41:7, 57:7, 64:16, 70:24, 73:20, 93:10, 98:5

[13] *The Holy Qur'an* 2:196-197

[14] *The Holy Qur'an* 9:123, 128, 119, 6, 74, 4:48, 89-90, 155, 11:19, 22, 16:106, 18:57

[15] *The Holy Qur'an* 11:110; 45:16, 3:3, 40:53, 2:122, 211, 246-248, 255, 5:12, 66, 70, 78-79

[16] *The Holy Qur'an* 3:3, 11:110, 40:53, 5:66, 23:49, 3:50, 87:14, 37:117-118, 46:10, 5:46, 48, 73:15, 48:29, 4:164

[17] *The Holy Qur'an* 2:122, 5:78-79

[18] *The Holy Qur'an* 6:83, 12:4-5, 9-10, 13, 15, 17-21, 23-25, 32-33, 35-38, 47-48, 51, 70, 93, 96

[19] *The Holy Qur'an* 33:7, 37:112, 6:89, 2:136, 19:51, 73:15, 4:164, 7:157-158, 4:163

[20] *The Holy Qur'an* 33:21, 11:31, 2:104, 3:153, 144

[21] *The Holy Qur'an* 33:40

[22] *The Holy Qur'an* 2:136, 6:89, 19:30, 33:7, 3:84, 2:136, 2:253, 3:45, 48-49, 4:171, 5:46, 110-111, 117, 6:85, 87, 89-90, 19:19, 42:13, 43:63, 57:27

[23] *The Holy Qur'an* 4:157-158

[24] *The Holy Qur'an* 6:164, 53:38

[25] *The Holy Qur'an* 3:48-49, 4:171, 5:46, 110, 6:85, 90

[26] *The Holy Qur'an* 4:4, 8, 11-12, 176

[27] *The Holy Qur'an* 2:187, 221-223, 226, 228-237, 3:15, 4:3, 12, 20, 22-24, 34-35, 129, 23:3, 101, 24:3, 26, 32-33. 33"37. 49, 36:56, 37:48, 40:8, 43:70, 44:54, 52:19, 57:27, 58:3-4, 60:10, 65:1-2, 4, 6

[28] *The Holy Qur'an* 2:228, 282, 3:35, 4:3-4, 11, 19, 24-25, 34, 176, 7:28, 31, 33, 12:23, 16:59, 23:3, 5, 33:31, 33, 50, 52-53, 55, 41:47, 42:11, 49, 53:27, 60:10

[29] *The Holy Qur'an* 67:15, 84:4, 58:18, 6:36, 20:55

[30] *The Holy Qur'an* 10:28, 45:26, 64:9, 56:7-12

[31] *The Holy Qur'an* 22:14, 23, 56, 32:19, 42:22, 43:72, 47:12, 48:5, 17, 51:15, 52:17, 54:54, 64:9, 65:11, 85:10

[32] *The Holy Qur'an* 4:10, 14, 56, 93, 115, 168, 7:18, 36, 8:14-15, 36-37, 9:17, 49, 63, 68, 72, 10:27, 11:16-17, 98, 106, 18:102, 106, 20:74, 22:51, 72, 24:57, 30:68, 32:20, 33:64, 35:36, 38:55, 39:32, 72, 45:10, 34, 46:34, 47:12, 48:6, 13, 50:24, 52:13, 56:45, 57:19, 58:17, 64:10, 66:9-10, 69:33-34, 49, 72:23, 76:31, 85:10, 92:14

[33] *The Holy Qur'an* 6:147

[34] *The Holy Qur'an* 26:68

[35] *The Holy Qur'an* 2:163, 59:22

[36] *The Holy Qur'an* 4:25, 129, 152, 48:14, 8:69

[37] *The Holy Qur'an* 7:167

[38] *The Holy Qur'an* 33:25

[39] *The Holy Qur'an* 2:106, 20, 109, 148, 3:29, 189, 5:17, 40, 8:41, 9:39, 18:45, 29:20, 33:27, 48:21, 59:6

[40] *The Holy Qur'an* 27:9

[41] *The Holy Qur'an* 42:9

[42] *The Holy Qur'an* 35:1

[43] *The Holy Qur'an* 58:7, 8:75, 24:64, 30:62, 48:26

[44] *The Holy Qur'an* 2:115

[45] *The Holy Qur'an* 44:6

[46] *The Holy Qur'an* 2:261

[47] *The Holy Qur'an* 42:25

[48] *The Holy Qur'an* 26:209

[49] *The Holy Qur'an* 8:51

[50] *The Holy Qur'an* 2:34, 38:73

[51] *The Holy Qur'an* 38:69

[52] *The Holy Qur'an* 2:34, 7:11, 17:61, 18:50, 38:73

[53] *The Holy Qur'an* 2:34

[54] *The Holy Qur'an* 38:73

[55] *The Holy Qur'an* 15:34, 7:13, 18, 15:34

[56] *The Holy Qur'an* 15:34

[57] *The Holy Qur'an* 4:163, 19:53

[58] *The Holy Qur'an* 4:163, 19:40, 33:7, 37:112

[59] *The Holy Qur'an* 4:163

[60] *The Holy Qur'an* 6:89

[61] *The Holy Qur'an* 6:89

[62] *The Holy Qur'an* 19:56

[63] *The Holy Qur'an* 4:163, 19:49

[64] *The Holy Qur'an* 4:163, 19;54

[65] *The Holy Qur'an* 4:163, 19:49, 4:155

[66] *The Holy Qur'an* 2:136, 4:163, 6:89, 33:7

[67] *The Holy Qur'an* 6:89

[68] *The Holy Qur'an* 4:163, 6:89

[69] *The Holy Qur'an* 6:89

[70] *The Holy Qur'an* 2:136, 19:51, 33:7, 73:15, 4:164

[71] *The Holy Qur'an* 7:157-158, 2:213, 5:19

[72] *The Holy Qur'an* 6:89

[73] *The Holy Qur'an* 33:40

[74] *The Holy Qur'an* 49:15

[75] *The Holy Qur'an* 4:59, 5:92, 24:54, 64:12

[76] *The Holy Qur'an* 3:30

[77] *The Holy Qur'an* 48:29

[78] *The Holy Qur'an* 42:3

[79] *The Holy Qur'an* 12:109

[80] *The Holy Qur'an* 26:208

[81] Reserved

[82] *The Book of Mormon: Another Testament of Jesus Christ,* Alma 40:11-14;

[83] *The Holy Qur'an* 7:40; *The Holy Qur'an* 13:35; *The Holy Qur'an* 7:40; *The Holy Qur'an* 57:21;

[84] *The Holy Qur'an* 57:11, 19; and, *The Holy Qur'an* 66:8;

[85] *The Holy Qur'an* 56:25-26;

[86] *The Holy Qur'an* 37:44; *The Holy Qur'an* 56:15-16, 34; *The Holy Qur'an* 38:51; *The Holy Qur'an* 52:19; *The Holy Qur'an* 18:31; *The Holy Qur'an* 55:76; and *The Holy Qur'an* 36:56;

[87] *The Holy Qur'an* 18:31; *The Holy Qur'an* 22:23; *The Holy Qur'an* 35:33; *The Holy Qur'an* 76:12, 21; and *The Holy Qur'an* 44:53;

[88] *The Holy Qur'an* 76:15; and *The Holy Qur'an* 56:18;

[89] *The Holy Qur'an* 25:24;

[90] *The Holy Qur'an* 55:76, 54;

[91] *The Holy Qur'an* 52:22; *The Holy Qur'an* 38:51; *The Holy Qur'an* 56:31, 33; *The Holy Qur'an* 36:56; *The Holy Qur'an* 41:30; *The Holy Qur'an* 55:54; *The Holy Qur'an* 69:23; *The Holy Qur'an* 13:35; *The Holy Qur'an* 44:55; *The Holy Qur'an* 56:33, 20; and *The Holy Qur'an* 37:42;

[92] *The Holy Qur'an* 55:68;

[93] *The Holy Qur'an* 38:51; *The Holy Qur'an* 76:5, 21, 17; *The Holy Qur'an* 69:24; *The Holy Qur'an* 37:46; *The Holy Qur'an* 77:43; and *The Holy Qur'an* 52:22;

[94] *The Holy Qur'an* 52:22; and *The Holy Qur'an* 56:21;

[95] *The Holy Qur'an* 13:35; and *The Holy Qur'an* 76:14;

[96] *The Holy Qur'an* 55:70, 58; *The Holy Qur'an* 52:19; *The Holy Qur'an* 44:54; *The Holy Qur'an* 56:22, 35; *The Holy Qur'an* 55:56, 74;

[97] *The Holy Qur'an* 78:33; and *The Holy Qur'an* 38:52;

[98] *The Holy Qur'an* 2:35; *The Holy Qur'an* 36:56; *The Holy Qur'an* 37:48; and *The Holy Qur'an* 40:8;

[99] *The Holy Qur'an* 55:66, and 50;

[100] *The Holy Qur'an* 78:32; *The Holy Qur'an* 9:22, 72, 100, 111, 89; *The Holy Qur'an* 7:43; *The Holy Qur'an* 10:9; *The Holy Qur'an* 13:35, 23; *The Holy Qur'an* 22:14, 23, 56; *The Holy Qur'an* 30:58, *The Holy Qur'an* 5:85, 119; *The Holy Qur'an* 58:22; *The Holy Qur'an* 65:11; *The Holy Qur'an* 25:10, 24; *The Holy Qur'an* 43:71-72; *The Holy Qur'an* 48:5, 17; *The Holy Qur'an* 57:12; *The Holy Qur'an* 88:10; *The Holy Qur'an* 98:8; *The Holy Qur'an* 25:16, 24; *The Holy Qur'an* 42:22; *The Holy Qur'an* 47:12, 14; *The Holy Qur'an* 44:52; *The Holy Qur'an* 54:54; *The Holy Qur'an* 51:15; *The Holy Qur'an* 52:17; *The Holy Qur'an* 48:5; *The Holy Qur'an* 32:19; *The Holy Qur'an* 64:9; *The Holy Qur'an* 85:10; *The Holy Qur'an* 55:46, 48, 50, 62, 64, 68, 66; *The Holy Qur'an* 38:50;

[101] *The Holy Qur'an* 47:14;

[102] *The Holy Qur'an* 57:13;

[103] *The Holy Qur'an* 56:35;

[104] *The Holy Qur'an* 2:35; *The Holy Qur'an* 36:56; *The Holy Qur'an* 37:48; *The Holy Qur'an* 40:8; *The Holy Qur'an* 52:19; and *The Holy Qur'an* 44:54;

[105] *The Holy Qur'an* 9:22; *The Holy Qur'an* 25:76; *The Holy Qur'an* 21:102; *The Holy Qur'an* 2:82; *The Holy Qur'an* 18:107; and *The Holy Qur'an* 39:73;

[106] *The Holy Qur'an* 29:9; *The Holy Qur'an* 76:8, 12; *The Holy Qur'an* 30:15; *The Holy Qur'an* 34:36; *The Holy Qur'an* 2:82; *The Holy Qur'an* 14:23; *The Holy Qur'an* 18:108; *The Holy Qur'an* 30:58; *The Holy Qur'an* 31:8; *The Holy Qur'an* 654:11; HUD 11:23;

[107] *The Holy Qur'an* 43:69;

[108] *The Holy Qur'an* 28:83;

[109] *The Holy Qur'an* 4:13, 57; *The Holy Qur'an* 42:22; *The Holy Qur'an* 18:30-31;

[110] *The Holy Qur'an* 3:133; *The Holy Qur'an* 39:73;

[111] *The Holy Qur'an* 38:49; and *The Holy Qur'an* 89:27;

[112] *The Holy Qur'an* 23:8;

[113] Reserved

[114] *The Holy Qur'an* 74:29; Man 76:4; *The Holy Qur'an* 101:9, *The Holy Qur'an* 111:2; *The Holy Qur'an* 73:12; *The Holy Qur'an* 25:11; *The Holy Qur'an* 85:10; *The Holy Qur'an* 92:17; *The Holy Qur'an* 2:39, 257; *The Holy Qur'an* 3:116, 131; *The Holy Qur'an* 10:27; *The Holy Qur'an* 43:74; The Cattle 6:128; Ornaments of Gold 43:75,77; The Most High 87:12; The Cave 18:53; The *The Holy Qur'an* 104:6; *The Holy Qur'an* 87:13; *The Holy Qur'an* 104:7; *The Holy Qur'an* 74:29; *The Holy Qur'an* 70:15; *The Holy Qur'an* 81:12; *The Holy Qur'an* 39:16; *The Holy Qur'an* 4:55-56; *The Holy Qur'an* 57:14; *The Holy Qur'an* 59:20; *The Holy Qur'an* 4:10; *The Holy Qur'an* 46:34; *The Holy Qur'an* 4:14; *The Holy Qur'an* 27:90; *The Holy Qur'an* 59:17; *The Holy Qur'an* 4:93, 115; *The Holy Qur'an* 85:10; and *The Holy Qur'an* 4:56;

[115] *The Holy Qur'an* 4:56;

[116] *The Holy Qur'an* 44:48;

[117] *The Holy Qur'an* 47:14; *The Holy Qur'an* 37:67; *The Holy Qur'an* 78:25;

[118] *The Holy Qur'an* 87:13;

[119] *The Holy Qur'an* 70:3;

[120] *The Holy Qur'an* 34:33; *The Holy Qur'an* 76:4; *The Holy Qur'an* 40:69; *The Holy Qur'an* 73:12;

[121] *The Holy Qur'an* 73:13; and *The Holy Qur'an* 69:36;

[122] *The Holy Qur'an* 56:52; and *The Holy Qur'an* 44:43, 46;

[123] *The Holy Qur'an* 56:42;

[124] *The Holy Qur'an* 70:18;

[125] *The Holy Qur'an* 74:46;

[126] *The Holy Qur'an* 70:17;

[127] *The Holy Qur'an* 76:4;

[128] *The Holy Qur'an* 38:85;

[129] *The Holy Qur'an* 58:17;

[130] *The Holy Qur'an* 4:10;

[131] *The Holy Qur'an* 7:36, *The Holy Qur'an* 45:10; *The Holy Qur'an* 4:56;

[132] *The Holy Qur'an* 11:17;

[133] *The Holy Qur'an* 4:168; *The Holy Qur'an* 8:15; *The Holy Qur'an* 9:72; *The Holy Qur'an* 24:57; *The Holy Qur'an* 30:68; *The Holy Qur'an* 35:36; *The Holy Qur'an* 39:32; *The Holy Qur'an* 57:19; *The Holy Qur'an* 66:9; *The Holy Qur'an* 69:49; *The Holy Qur'an* 92:14; *The Holy Qur'an* 8:36; *The Holy Qur'an* 39:72; and *The Holy Qur'an* 9:49;

[134] *The Holy Qur'an* 11:16;

[135] *The Holy Qur'an* 69:33;

[136] *The Holy Qur'an* 72:23; and *The Holy Qur'an* 4:14;

[137] *The Holy Qur'an* 85:10;

[138] *The Holy Qur'an* 10:27;

[139] *The Holy Qur'an* 20:74;

[140] *The Holy Qur'an* 4:93;

[141] *The Holy Qur'an* 69:49; and *The Holy Qur'an* 57:19;

[142] *The Holy Qur'an* 78:21;

[143] *The Holy Qur'an* 38:55;

[144] *The Holy Qur'an* 76:31;

[145] *The Holy Qur'an* 9:68, 72; *The Holy Qur'an* 48:6; *The Holy Qur'an* 66:9;

[146] *The Holy Qur'an* 9:17; *The Holy Qur'an* 48:6;

[147] *The Holy Qur'an* 50:24;

[148] *The Holy Qur'an* 111:2;

[149] *The Holy Qur'an* 2:39, 257; *The Holy Qur'an* 3:116, 131; *The Holy Qur'an* 41:28; *The Holy Qur'an* 42:45; *The Holy Qur'an* 6:128; *The Holy Qur'an* 11:108, and 113;

[150] *The Holy Qur'an* 74:43-44;

[151] *The Holy Qur'an* 92:14;

[152] *The Holy Qur'an* 92:17;

[153] *The Holy Qur'an* 6:128

Endnotes—Chapter 6, Modern Prophets

[1] *The Holy Qur'an* 33:40

[2] *Modern Prophets, Ensign*, May 2020, NLA, 5, (29.30 When); *Modern Prophets, Doctrine & Covenants, 1:20*; *Modern Prophets, Ensign*, May 2017, JRH, 2, (15:15 I), RMN, 1 (31.31); *Modern Prophets, Ensign*, May 2018, RMN, 4, (40.40 This); *Modern Prophets, Ensign*, May 2019, MRB, 2, (29.29 I); *Modern Prophets, Ensign*, Nov 2011, RMN, 5, (21.21 God); *Modern Prophets, Ensign*, Nov 2012, RMN, 1, (8.28 The); *Modern Prophets, Ensign*, Nov 2012, DFU, 1, (17.64 First); *Modern Prophets, Ensign*, Nov 2015, DTC, 5, (4.23 Following); *Modern Prophets, Ensign*, Nov 2019, RMN, 4, (40.40 I); *Modern Prophets, Liahona*, Nov 2021, DHO, 1, (16.25 Another)

[3] *Modern Prophets, Doctrine & Covenants*, 34:6, 65:3-4; *Modern Prophets, Ensign*, May 2014, DFU, 3, (57.57 Let), NLA, 1, (39.40); *Modern Prophets, Ensign*, May 2016, RMN, 3, (27.27 My); *Modern Prophets, Ensign*, May 2017, DFU, 4, (42.57 Brothers, 43.57 We); *Modern Prophets, Ensign*, May 2018, QLC, 5, (4.33 One), RMN, 3-2, (24.24 Now); *Modern Prophets, Ensign*, May 2019, DTC, 4, (11.21 What, 13.21 In, 18.21 Also, 21.21 This, 3.21 In, 7.21 So, 9.21 While); *Modern Prophets, Ensign*, May 2020, DAB, 4, (12.38 The), DHO, 5, (2.22 We), DTC, 5, (26.26 We), RAR, 4 (10.25), RMN, 4-1, (38.50 Now, 47.50 With); *Modern Prophets, Ensign*, Nov 2011, DAB, 2, (9.28 The); *Modern Prophets, Ensign*, Nov 2013, NLA, 5, (39.39 As); *Modern Prophets, Ensign*, Nov 2017, MRB, 5, (2.35 By), RMN, 2 (40.42 I); *Modern Prophets, Ensign*, Nov 2018, HBE, 3, (27.27 You), QLC, 1 (18.39 President), RMN, 4 (33.35 My), RMN, WS (32.33 I); *Modern Prophets, Ensign*, Nov 2019, RAR, 2, (20.22 What), RMN, 2 (5.9 You), RMN, 3 (20.32 We), RMN, 5 (3.22 Of); *Modern Prophets, Ensign*, Nov 2020, HBE, 3, (2.26 As), RMN, 5 (10.10 May); *Modern Prophets, Liahona*, May 2021, HBE, 3, (21.23 It), RMN, 1, (10.12 Part); RMN, 3, (11.27 You); *Modern Prophets, Liahona*, May 2022, RMN, 5, (10.11 These); *Modern Prophets, Liahona*, Nov 2021, RMN, 1, (9.10 This); *Modern Prophets, Liahona*, Nov 2022, RMN, 4, (29.31 As, 30.31 I)

⁴ *Modern Prophets, Doctrine & Covenants*, 76:23, 6:21; *Modern Prophets, Liahona,* May 2013, TSM, 3, (38.39 Of); *Modern Prophets, Ensign,* May 2014, BKP, 5, (22.33 In); *Modern Prophets, Ensign,* May 2014, BKP, 5, (32.33 I); *Modern Prophets, Ensign,* May 2015, BKP, 1, (25.27 I); *Modern Prophets, Ensign,* May 2015, JRH, 5, (15.18 That), TSM, 4, (21.21 May); *Modern Prophets, Ensign,* May 2016, DHO, 5, (3.26 The); *Modern Prophets, Ensign,* May 2016, HBE, 1, (27.28 I); *Modern Prophets, Ensign,* May 2017, DHO, 4, (19.27 To); *Modern Prophets, Ensign,* May 2020, N, 4-1, (39.50 We); *Modern Prophets, Ensign,* May 2020, DTC, 5, (25.26 Joseph); *Modern Prophets, Ensign,* May 2020, DHO, 5, (1.22 Even); *Modern Prophets, Ensign,* May 2020, RAR, 4, (14.25 I); *Modern Prophets, Ensign,* May 2020, DFU, 5, (1.62 My); *Modern Prophets, Ensign,* May 2020, DTC, 5, (25.26 Joseph); *Modern Prophets, Ensign,* Nov 2011, DHO, 5, (29.29 Jesus); *Modern Prophets, Ensign,* Nov 2011, DHO, 5, (3.29 Jesus); *Modern Prophets, Ensign,* Nov 2012, TSM, 3, (42.43 Of); *Modern Prophets, Ensign,* Nov 2014, DAB, 5, (28.30 Absolute); *Modern Prophets, Ensign,* Nov 2014, HBE, 3, (38.38 I); *Modern Prophets, Ensign,* Nov 2014, HBE, 4, (37.39 I); *Modern Prophets, Ensign,* Nov 2015, NLA, 3, (16.28 Both); *Modern Prophets, Ensign,* Nov 2015, NLA, 3, (16.28 Both); *Modern Prophets, Ensign,* Nov 2015, DGR, 4, (9.10 With); *Modern Prophets, Ensign,* Nov 2015, DAB, 5, (43.49 I); *Modern Prophets, Ensign,* Nov 2017, DAB, 4, (32.32 I); *Modern Prophets, Ensign,* Nov 2017, RMN, 2, (41.41 I); *Modern Prophets, Ensign,* Nov 2019, JRH, 1, (14.16 One); *Modern Prophets, Ensign,* Nov 2019, NLA, 5, (37.37 I); *Modern Prophets, Ensign,* Nov 2020, DAB, 1, (29.29 I); *Modern Prophets, Ensign,* Nov 2020, DTC, 2, (22.28 The); *Modern Prophets, Ensign,* Nov 2020, DAB, 1, (29.29 I); *Modern Prophets, Liahona,* May 2021, US, 4, (14.14 My); *Modern Prophets, Liahona,* May 2021, US, 4, (4.14 Jesus); *Modern Prophets, Liahona,* Nov 2021, MRB, 3, (31.31 I); *Modern Prophets, Liahona,* Nov 2021, DFU, 4, (3.48 We); *Modern Prophets, Liahona,* Nov 2021, MRB, 3, (31.31 I); *Modern Prophets, Liahona,* Nov 2021, NLA, 5, (42.42 I)

⁵ *Modern Prophets, Pearl of Great Price, JS--History,* 1:17; *Modern Prophets, Ensign,* May 2013, RMN, 2, (14.21 Our); *Modern Prophets,*

Ensign, Nov 2014, NLA, 2, (35.36 I); *Modern Prophets, Ensign,* Nov 2014, NLA, 2, (7.36 Joseph); *Modern Prophets, Ensign,* May 2015, MRB, 3, (37.38 On); *Modern Prophets, Ensign,* Nov 2015, DGR, 4, (10.10 I); *Modern Prophets, Ensign,* Nov 2016, HBE, 4, (40.40 I); *Modern Prophets, Ensign,* May 2017, DHO, 4, (1.27 Our); *Modern Prophets, Ensign,* May 2017, HBE, 3, (21.21 I); *Modern Prophets, Ensign,* May 2017, TSM, 4, (3.6 We); *Modern Prophets, Ensign,* Nov 2017, HBE, 4, (3.36 Like); *Modern Prophets, Ensign,* Nov 2019, GES, 4, (32.39 I); *Modern Prophets, Ensign,* Nov 2019, HBE, 3, (21.21 I); *Modern Prophets, Ensign,* Nov 2019, JRH, 1, (14.16 One); *Modern Prophets, Ensign,* Nov 2019, RMN, 5, (14.22 Now); *Modern Prophets, Ensign,* May 2020, DAB, 4, (1.38 In); *Modern Prophets, Ensign,* May 2020, DAB, 4, (38.38 I); *Modern Prophets, Ensign,* May 2020, DHO, 5, (1.22 Even); *Modern Prophets, Ensign,* May 2020, GWG, 3, (9.25 Latter-day); *Modern Prophets, Ensign,* May 2020, RAR, 4, (1.25 My); *Modern Prophets, Ensign,* May 2020, RMN, 3, (2.29 My); *Modern Prophets, Ensign,* May 2020, N, 4-1, (41.50 In); *Modern Prophets, Ensign,* Nov 2020, QLC, 1, (15.36 It); May 2021, DFU, 1, (33.62 Two); *Modern Prophets, Liahona,* Nov 2022, DAB, 4, (25.25 I); *Modern Prophets, Liahona,* Nov 2022, MRB, 2, (10.28 As)

[6] *Modern Prophets, Pearl of Great Price, JS--History,* 1:11-13

[7] *Modern Prophets, Pearl of Great Price, JS--History,* 1:17; *Modern Prophets, Ensign,* Nov 2022, MRB, 2, (10.28 As); *Modern Prophets, Ensign,* Nov 2014, NLA, 2, (35.36 I); *Modern Prophets, Ensign,* Nov 2014, NLA, 2, (7.36 Joseph); *Modern Prophets, Ensign,* May 2015, MRB, 3, (37.38 On); *Modern Prophets, Ensign,* Nov 2015, DGR, 4, (10.10 I); *Modern Prophets, Ensign,* Nov 2016, HBE, 4, (40.40 I); *Modern Prophets, Ensign,* May 2017, DHO, 4, (1.27 Our); *Modern Prophets, Ensign,* May 2017, HBE, 3, (21.21 I); *Modern Prophets, Ensign,* Nov 2017, HBE, 4, (3.36 Like); *Modern Prophets, Ensign,* Nov 2017, HBE, 4, (3.36 Like); *Modern Prophets, Ensign,* Nov 2019, GES, 4, (32.39 I); *Modern Prophets, Ensign,* Nov 2019, HBE, 3, (21.21 I); *Modern Prophets, Ensign,* Nov 2019, RMN, 5, (14.22 Now); *Modern Prophets, Ensign,* May 2020, DAB, 4, (1.38 In); *Modern Prophets, Ensign,* May 2020, DAB, 4, (38.38 I); *Modern Prophets, Ensign,* May 2020, GWG, 3, (9.25 Latter-day); *Modern Prophets,*

Ensign, May 2020, RMN, 3, (2.29 My); *Modern Prophets, Ensign,* May 2020, N, 4-1, (41.50 In); *Modern Prophets, Liahona,* May 2021, DFU, 1, (33.62 Two); *Modern Prophets, Liahona,* Nov 2022, DAB, 4, (25.25 I); *Modern Prophets, Liahona,* Nov 2022, MRB, 2, (10.28 As); *Modern Prophets, Ensign,* May 2020, DHO, 5, (1.22 Even); *Modern Prophets, Ensign,* Nov 2020, QLC, 1, (15.36 It); *Modern Prophets, Ensign,* Nov 2019, JRH, 1, (14.16 One); *Modern Prophets, Ensign,* May 2017, TSM, 4, (3.6 We); *Modern Prophets, Ensign,* May 2020, RAR, 4, (1.25 My); *Modern Prophets, Ensign,* May 2013, RMN, 2, (14.21 Our)

[8] *Modern Prophets, Pearl of Great Price, JS--History,* 1:26

[9] *Modern Prophets, Pearl of Great Price, JS--History,* 1:18-20

[10] *Modern Prophets, Doctrine & Covenants,* 1:30; *Modern Prophets, Ensign,* Nov 2017, HBE, 4, (35.36 I); *Modern Prophets, Ensign,* Nov 2017, NLA, 5, (28.55 President); *Modern Prophets, Ensign,* May 2016, HBE, 1, (28.28 This); *Modern Prophets, Ensign,* May 2017, TSM, 4, (5.6 If); *Modern Prophets, Ensign,* May 2017, TSM, 4, (5.6 If); *Modern Prophets, Ensign,* Nov 2018, DTC, 2, (9.24 In)

[11] *Modern Prophets, Liahona,* Nov 2022, MRB, 2, (10.28 As); *Modern Prophets, Ensign, May* 2020, RMN, 4-1, (35.50 That); *Modern Prophets, Ensign, Nov 2012,* NLA, 2, (6.31 Our)

[12] *Modern Prophets, Liahona,* Nov 2022, MRB, 2, (10.28 As)

[13] *Modern Prophets, Ensign, Nov 2015,* DTC, 5, (21.23 Its, and f.n. 4 The)

[14] *Modern Prophets, Doctrine & Covenants,* 34:6, 65:3-4; *Modern Prophets, Ensign,* May 2014, DFU, 3, (57.57 Let); *Modern Prophets, Ensign,* May 2014, NLA, 1, (39.40 As); *Modern Prophets, Ensign,* May 2017, DFU, 4, (42.57 Brothers); *Modern Prophets, Ensign,* May 2017, DFU, 4, (43.57 We); *Modern Prophets, Ensign,* May 2018, N, 3-2, (24.24 Now); *Modern Prophets, Ensign,* May 2018, QLC, 5, (4.33 One); *Modern Prophets, Ensign,* May 2019, DTC, 4, (11.21 What); *Modern Prophets, Ensign,* May 2019, DTC, 4, (13.21 In); *Modern Prophets, Ensign,* May 2019, DTC, 4, (18.21 Also); *Modern Prophets, Ensign,* May 2019, DTC, 4, (21.21 This); *Modern Prophets, Ensign,* May 2019, DTC, 4, (3.21 In); *Modern Prophets, Ensign,* May 2019,

DTC, 4, (7.21 So); *Modern Prophets, Ensign,* May 2019, DTC, 4, (9.21 While); *Modern Prophets, Ensign,* May 2020, DAB, 4, (12.38 The); *Modern Prophets, Ensign,* May 2020, DHO, 5, (2.22 We); *Modern Prophets, Ensign,* May 2020, N, 4-1, (38.50 Now); *Modern Prophets, Ensign,* May 2020, N, 4-1, (47.50 With); *Modern Prophets, Ensign,* May 2020, RAR, 4, (10.25 We); *Modern Prophets, Ensign,* May 2021, HBE, 3, (21.23 It); *Modern Prophets, Ensign,* May 2021, RMN, 1, (10.12 Part); *Modern Prophets, Ensign,* May 2021, RMN, 3, (11.27 You); *Modern Prophets, Ensign,* May 2022, RMN, 5, (10.11 These); *Modern Prophets, Ensign,* Nov 2011, DAB, 2, (9.28 The); *Modern Prophets, Ensign,* Nov 2013, NLA, 5, (39.39 As); *Modern Prophets, Ensign,* Nov 2017, MRB, 5, (2.35 By); *Modern Prophets, Ensign,* Nov 2017, RMN, 2, (40.42 I); *Modern Prophets, Ensign,* Nov 2018, HBE, 3, (27.27 You); *Modern Prophets, Ensign,* Nov 2018, MN, WS, (32.33 I); *Modern Prophets, Ensign,* Nov 2018, QLC, 1, (18.39 President); *Modern Prophets, Ensign,* Nov 2018, RMN, 4, (33.35 My); *Modern Prophets, Ensign,* Nov 2019, RAR, 2, (20.22 What); *Modern Prophets, Ensign,* Nov 2019, RMN, 2, (5.9 You); *Modern Prophets, Ensign,* Nov 2019, RMN, 3, (20.32 We); *Modern Prophets, Ensign,* Nov 2019, RMN, 5, (3.22 Of); *Modern Prophets, Ensign,* Nov 2020, HBE, 3, (2.26 As); *Modern Prophets, Ensign,* Nov 2020, RMN, 5, (10.10 May); *Modern Prophets, Liahona,* Nov 2022, RMN, 4, (29.31 As); *Modern Prophets, Liahona,* Nov 2021, RMN, 1, (9.10 This)

[15] *Modern Prophets, Ensign,* May 2019, DTC, 4 (1.21 In); *Modern Prophets, Liahona,* Nov 2021, MRB, 3, (14.31In)

[16] *Modern Prophets, Ensign,* May 2019, DTC, 4 (21.21 This); *Modern Prophets, Liahona,* Nov, 2022, GWG, 4 (28.30 The); *Modern Prophets, Doctrine & Covenants,* 29:11; *Modern Prophets, Pearl of Great Price, Moses,* 7:64

[17] *Modern Prophets, Doctrine & Covenants,* 88:97; *Modern Prophets, Ensign,* May 2016, HBE, 1 (27:28 I); *Modern Prophets, Ensign,* May 2019, DTC, 4 (18.21 Also); *Modern Prophets, Ensign,* May 2019, DTC, 5 (25:26 Joseph); *Modern Prophets, Ensign,* Nov 2017, RMN, 2 (41:41 I); *Modern Prophets, Ensign,* May 2016, HBE, 2 (7:23 The); *Modern Prophets, Liahona,* Nov, 2021, RMN, 5 (8:12 Nothing); *Modern Prophets, Pearl of Great Price, Moses,* 7:53

[18] *Modern Prophets, Ensign,* May, 2012, QLC, 2 (17.25 The)

[19] *Modern Prophets, Ensign,* Nov, 2017, RMN, 2 (41:41 I)

[20] *Modern Prophets, Liahona,* May, 2021, US, 4 (14:14 My)

[21] *Modern Prophets, Ensign,* May, 2018 MRB, 1 (29.33 As)

[22] *Modern Prophets, Doctrine & Covenants,* 19:18, 76:107, 88:106, 133:50; *Modern Prophets, Ensign,* May, 2014 RDH, 2 (23.25 Obedience); *Modern Prophets, Ensign,* May, 2015 JRH, 5 (15.18 That) and QLC, 2, (35.38 If); *Modern Prophets, Ensign,* May, 2018 DAB, 2 (28.34 Jesus, and 29.34 The), DFU, 5 (10.65 To), and RMN, 4 (1.40 What); *Modern Prophets, Ensign,* May, 2019 JRH, 2 (9.16 May); *Modern Prophets, Ensign,* Nov, 2011 RDH, 4 (26.27 Such); *Modern Prophets, Ensign,* Nov, 2012 BKP, 4 (23.31 We); *Modern Prophets, Ensign,* Nov, 2014 BKP, 1 (13.26 The); *Modern Prophets, Ensign,* Nov, 2017 QLC, 2 (10.34); *Modern Prophets, Ensign,* Nov, 2018 HBE, 5 (5.29 My); *Modern Prophets, Ensign,* Nov, 2018 RMN, 4 (13.35 Consider); *Modern Prophets, Ensign,* Nov, 2020, HBE, 5 (17.32 When)

[23] *Modern Prophets, Ensign,* Nov, 2012, BKP, 4 (23.31 We); *Modern Prophets, Ensign,* May, 2015, QLC, 2 (35.38 If); *Modern Prophets, Ensign,* Nov, 2016 RAR, 5 (7.32 Jesus); *Modern Prophets, Ensign,* Nov, 2017 QLC, 2 (10.34 The); *Modern Prophets, Ensign,* Nov, 2018 HBE, 5 (5.29 My)

[24] *Modern Prophets, Ensign,* Nov, 2018 RMN, 4 (13.35 Consider); *Modern Prophets, Ensign,* May, 2019, JRH, 2 (9.16 May); *Modern Prophets, Ensign,* May, 2021 RMN, 4 (16.33 First); *Modern Prophets, Ensign,* May, 2020 DHO, 5 (3.22 All); *Modern Prophets, Ensign,* May, 2012 NLA, 5 (30.30 I); *Modern Prophets, Ensign,* May, 2015, MRB, 3, (36.38 Through); *Modern Prophets, Ensign,* Nov 2016, MRB, 4, (16.34 Where); *Modern Prophets, Ensign,* May 2018, DFU, 5, (23.65 Jesus); *Modern Prophets, Ensign,* Nov 2018, HBE, 5, (5.29 My); *Modern Prophets, Ensign,* Nov 2020, DTC, 2, (22.28 The); *Modern Prophets, Ensign,* Nov 2021, DAB, 2, (19.21 As); *Modern Prophets, Ensign,* May 2022, RAR, 4, (41.41 I); *Modern Prophets, Ensign,* Nov 2022, HBE, 5, (21.24 Jesus)

[25] *Modern Prophets, Ensign,* Nov 2013, HBE, 4, (32.36 Heavenly)

²⁶ *Modern Prophets, Ensign,* Nov 2018, HBE, 5, (5.29 My)

²⁷ *Modern Prophets, Liahona,* May 2021, DHO, 4, (12.25 Our)

²⁸ *Modern Prophets, Ensign,* May 2018, DFU, 5, (10.65 To)

²⁹ *Modern Prophets, Liahona,* May 2021, US, 4, (9.14 In)

³⁰ *Modern Prophets, Liahona,* Nov 2016, MRB, 4, (16.34 Where)

Endnotes—Chapter 7, Sutra Pitaka (Limited)

[1] *Sutra Pitakas, Anattalakkhana,* (38:46 Any), (41:46 Any), (5:46 Mental)

[2] *Sutra Pitakas, Anattalakkhana,* (3:46 Feeling), (37:46 Thus), (5:46 Mental), (2:46 The)

[3] *Sutra Pitakas,* Dhammakakkappavattana, (4:29 What), (8:29 Now)

[4] *Sutra Pitakas, Anattalakkhana,* (44:46 With), (38:46 Any), (41:46 Any), (40:46 Any)

[5] *Sutra Pitakas,* Dhammakakkappavattana, (5:29 Now)

[6] *Sutra Pitakas, Anattalakkhana,* (44:46 With); *Sutra Pitakas,* Dhammakakkappavattana, (23:29 And)

[7] *Sutra Pitakas,* Adittapariyaya, (2.14 Monks), (7.14 The), (6.14 The), (3.14 The), (5.14 The), (4.14 The)

[8] *Sutra Pitakas, Anattalakkhana,* (46:46 And), (43.46 Seeing)

[9] https://www.khanacademy.org/humanities/ap-art-history/introduction-cultures-religions-apah/buddhism-apah/a/the-historical-buddha

[10] *Sutra Pitakas,* Dhammakakkappavattana, (26:29 And), (27.29 And), (N27.2)

[11] *Sutra Pitakas, Anattalakkhana,* (44:46 With)

[12] *Sutra Pitakas, Anattalakkhana,* (43:46 Seeing)

[13] *Sutra Pitakas,* Dhammakakkappavattana, (23:29 And)

[14] *Sutra Pitakas, Anattalakkhana,* (33:46 And)

[15] *Sutra Pitakas, Anattalakkhana,* (7:46 How)

[16] *Sutra Pitakas, Anattalakkhana,* (31:46 How)

[17] *Sutra Pitakas, Anattalakkhana,* (13:46 How)

[18] *Sutra Pitakas, Anattalakkhana,* (25:46 How)

[19] *Sutra Pitakas, Anattalakkhana,* (19:46 How)

[20] *Sutra Pitakas,* Dhammakakkappavattana, (4:29 What), (8:29 Now)

[21] *Sutra Pitakas, Anattalakkhana,* (43:46 Seeing); Dhammakakkappavattana, (6:29 Now); Dhammakakkappavattana, (N6.4); Dhammakakkappavattana, (5:29 Now);

[22] Dhammakakkappavattana, (N6.4)

[23] *Sutra Pitakas, Anattalakkhana,* (43:46 Seeing)

[24] Dhammakakkappavattana, (27.29 And)

[25] Dhammakakkappavattana, (6.29 Now); Dhammakakkappavattana, (N6.4); Dhammakakkappavattana, (5.29 Now); *Sutra Pitakas, Anattalakkhana,* (43:46 Seeing)

[26] *Anattalakkhana,* (45:46 That); Dhammakakkappavattana, (29.29 Then)

[27] *Anattalakkhana,* (41:46 Any); *Anattalakkhana,* (38:46 Any); *Anattalakkhana,* (40:46 Any)

[28] Dhammakakkappavattana, (10.29 And-20.29 And), (23.29 And), (9.29 That)

[29] *Anattalakkhana,* (41:46 Any); *Anattalakkhana,* (38:46 Any); *Anattalakkhana,* (40:46 Any)

[30] *Anattalakkhana,* (43:46 Seeing)

[31] Dhammakakkappavattana, (6.29 Now); Dhammakakkappavattana, (N6.4); Dhammakakkappavattana, (5.29 Now); *Sutra Pitakas, Anattalakkhana,* (43:46 Seeing)

www.ingramcontent.com/pod-product-compliance
Ingram Content Group UK Ltd.
Pitfield, Milton Keynes, MK11 3LW, UK
UKHW020244240426
12048UKWH00026B/1608